GW00724559

TWO FAMILIES

AND THE

GREAT WAR

BY TOM TYLER

With All Good Wishes,

JACK OF ALL TRADES PUBLISHING

WRITTEN, PRINTED AND PUBLISHED IN ENGLAND
2017

First published in Great Britain in 2017

British Library Cataloguing-in-Publication Data.
A CIP record for this title is available from the British Library.

ISBN 978-0-9567463-3-7

Published by Jack of All Trades Publishing,
32 The Limes, Ipswich, Suffolk. IP5 1EA. U.K.

Printed by The Lavenham Press,
Arbons House, 47 Water St. Lavenham, Suffolk CO109RN U.K.

Cover design by Tom Tyler

CONTENTS

FRONTISPIECE

INTRODUCTION AND ACKNOWLEDGEMENTS

FOREWORD

DEDICATION AND BIBLIOGRAPHY.

INTRODUCTION.

This book, "Two families and the Great War" and the effect of that war on them, is in particular an account of the seven family members who went to fight in the war, four of whom never returned home to their families. Their graves are to be found in different areas of France.

In common with millions of their comrades, and enemies, those who did return home said very little about their experiences. They wiped the horror, pain and sorrow from their memories, because it was the only way they could cope. Their families respected their silence, and quietly grieved with them, while helping them to rebuild their lives as best they could. My father was typical of these returned soldiers.

By 2015 Commemorations of the events of 100 years before were well under way, and after being given details of a Bed and Breakfast run by an English couple, and situated in the centre of the Somme Battlefield, I felt I should make the effort to go there. We still had no idea at all where our family members had served. I also felt I should try to find out a bit more, and via a website was put in touch with a researcher. I learned that because of the Centenary, and greatly increased interest, a lot of service records which had hitherto not seen the light of day were being dusted down and made available to researchers. It was still quite a challenge, however, to find what you wanted.

Nine days before we were due to make our trip, my printer spewed out 125 A4 pages, including my father's medical certificate dated August 1914, - he was declared "Fit", and 105 pages of the War Diary of the 92nd Company, Royal Engineers, from 1915 to 1917. My father, Oliver Tyler joined as a 2nd Lieutenant in early 1915, and rose by 1917 to be Commanding Officer. I sat in my armchair learning where he was based, exactly what his duties and challenges were, and reading pages written in his unmistakeable handwriting, and bearing his signature. I learned more in a couple of days than we, his family, had known in the last 100 years.

Railways and horses made a huge contribution to transport in the Great War

Moreover, we discovered that our Bed and Breakfast was in the middle of the area where my father, and his brother Roland had served, and that most of the places named in the diary were within easy cycling distance, - or a ride on horseback, from the place where we would be staying. We were even able to find the railway my father and his engineers built to take materials up to the front for the forthcoming battle of the Somme on 1st July 1916. The trains are still steam hauled today, and we rode up to the front on one of them.

A full account of our visit would fill another book, but seeing the places today helped greatly to visualise what it must have been like, and it also spurred me on to make use of Lawrence, our researcher, to find out more about the other six men. It also turned out that our host in France, John, is a great expert on the First World War, with an extensive library, and he was a great help to us, even finding more information for us on his computer. We really were unbelievably lucky with our whole expedition, as well as having very helpful and perceptive companions.

For many years I have been the family archivist, - mainly because no-one else wanted to do it! – and so I had already in my possession a lot of old family photographs dating back to about the 1870s. Many are reproduced in this book. But in the autumn of 2015 we returned for a holiday to the old family holiday spot at East Portlemouth, opposite Salcombe in South Devon. This was a place beloved of both my father, Oliver Tyler, and my Uncle Roland, who lived there with his family, and this was where his unmarried daughter, Shirley, died about fifteen years ago. We were never given any family papers at all.

I decided, after meeting up with two friends of my childhood days, to pay a visit to the people who now lived in what had been Shirley's cottage. They were most kind, and did remember there might have been some papers in a black bag in the cellar, afflicted by damp at some time.

Later that day a carrier bag arrived on the doorstep, containing eight photograph albums and my uncle Roland's Record of Service for the War. I felt incredibly excited, and that another large piece of the jigsaw puzzle had fallen into place! What made this find most valuable was that Roland Tyler, as a Dispatch Rider, carried a camera around with him. I think that was strictly against regulations, but thank goodness he did!

I have felt strongly that the record of these seven men should be told, as they symbolise and represent the millions of others who fought, and who either died or survived, albeit often greatly changed, and whose families were called on to suffer with them, often for the rest of their lives. There is no glamour to war, and I have been blest with a lifetime of peace, which I hope will be the blessing my children and grandchildren also experience. But we must never forget those who answered the call to fight out of a deep sense of comradeship and duty, and whose sacrifice, - in two world wars, preserved our freedom as a nation.

Tom Tyler

FOREWORD.

Throughout 2014, 2015 and 2016 there have been so many agonising reminders of the sheer enormity of the trench warfare of a hundred years ago, and no doubt these will continue throughout 2017 and 2018. Inevitably, perhaps, the emphasis has been on the grotesque scale of the human devastation and loss of life. As a result, it has been all too easy to lose sight of the immediate and longer term impact on individuals and families. History naturally chronicles the broad sweep of events, but the personal element has a place too, if we are to appreciate fully the significance of those events, and how they continue to affect our own lives.

This is where this slim volume fulfils a real need. The painstaking research that enables us to follow, with newly discovered detail and fascinating photos, the mixed fortunes of seven men through those years is obviously of considerable interest for those who have a family connection with them. However, their collective experience will be of wider significance, because it also provides an evocative illustration of the effect of the "Great War" on real people, real families and thus the real world we can all relate to.

Paul Tyler

ACKNOWLEDGEMENTS.

This book has been very much a team effort, and first I must thank Lawrence Woodcock, the researcher who found so much information for us, and also John and Jenny Knight, who helped us greatly during our visit to the Somme battlefield in France, and our companions, Ann and Diana Mason

Many members of the Tyler family have provided information, help and encouragement. Among these I want to mention Jennifer Tyler, Norman Tyler, Judy Crimes, Tim Tyler, Mary Webb, Oliver Tyler, Dr. Andrew Tyler, Lord Paul Tyler, Rev. John Tyler, Paul D. Tyler. Without their help this book would never have been written.

My computer skills seem to deteriorate over time, and a younger generation has been called in to help with pictures. I am especially grateful to Stacey-Anne Penny, Natalie Harris and Max Slater-Robins for help sorting out tangles and teaching new skills, and particularly Philip Tyler for final editing.

The paintings reproduced on pages 7, 14, 18 and 24 are by Malcolm Root, FGRA, and I am most grateful for his permission to reproduce them.

As usual, my wife 'Tricia has been an invaluable proof reader and critic!

BOOKS BY THE SAME AUTHOR.

British Jigsaw Puzzles of the 20th Century.   Published by Richard Dennis Publications.
Malcolm Root's Transport Paintings. The Railway Paintings of Malcolm Root.
A Pageant of Transport. Malcolm Root. All published by Halsgrove.
When Motoring was Fun. When Holidays were Fun. Published by Halsgrove.
Fifteen Love, a book of short and tall stories. Published by Jack of All Trades Publishing.
A Cancer Patients Handbook. Published by Jack of All Trades Publishing.

All the above books available from the author, at 32 The Limes, Ipswich IP5 1EA.

DEDICATION

*This book is dedicated to all those men and women
who served in the Great War 1914 to 1918,
and especially those who gave their lives for others.
We shall remember them.*

BIBLIOGRAPHY

Into Battle. A Soldier's Diary of the Great War. by John Glubb.
A fascinating and detailed account of the period during which Oliver Tyler, a fellow Royal Engineer, served in exactly the same area of the Somme.

War Diary of the 92nd Company, Royal Engineers. Supplied by Forces Records.

CHAPTER 1. EUROPE, 1900 TO 1914

Queen Victoria pictured towards the end of her reign

In January 1901, Queen Victoria lay propped up in her great bed at Osborne House, on the Isle of Wight. Her breathing was shallow, for at last, after ruling for sixty four years, the great Queen was dying. Around her bed, and in rooms and corridors throughout the house, family, friends and servants waited in awe and doubt. Most had never known any other sovereign. The lives of many of them had been controlled by this extraordinary little lady.

Closest to Victoria were two male relatives. On her left knelt Kaiser Wilhelm II, Emperor of Germany, holding her left hand in his right. It had to be like that, as the Kaisers left hand and arm had been deformed since birth, and he was very sensitive regarding this disability. Opposite him knelt Alexandra, Princess of Wales, holding the dying queen's right hand. Beside her was the Queen's eldest son, and the heir to the throne, Albert Edward, known to all as Bertie. Kneeling was quite a challenge for Bertie due to his weight problem. Wilhelm was Queen Victoria's eldest grandson, so the two were uncle and nephew.

The scene was not only remarkable in that it signalled the end of a long and eventful reign, - the longest in English history so far, but it was also hugely significant that around the bedside were men and women who would play a dominant role in European affairs during the next twenty years and more. When Wilhelm arrived at Victoria Station in London, having heard the news that his grandmother did not have long to live, he was quite surprised to be met by his uncle Bertie, and by no means sure of his reception. The Germans had openly sided with the Boers in South Africa in the present war, and even supplied them with arms.

Wilhelm, looking very sheepish, had said "Uncle Bertie, I have to tell you that I come here simply as my mother's son."

Bertie had given him a very cordial welcome, and in the great Queens bedroom the family were totally united. After her death Wilhelm was given a prominent place in the funeral ceremonies, and he showed his gratitude towards the new King Emperor Edward VII. But Wilhelm was a very complex and unbalanced character, much inclined to illogical jealousies and suspicions. When surrounded by his family he was one person, but was quite a different one when back in Germany surrounded by toadies and militarists. His attitude to the Boer War had been typical.

An effigy of President Kruger made by the Tyler boys

One must admit that the whole Boer problem in South Africa had been a disaster for the British. Throughout the world, and especially in Europe and the United States, there was great jealousy towards the power, influence and trading success of the British Empire. Many other countries were desperate to emulate Britain's role in the world, and looked askance at all the countries coloured red on the world map. With the usual preference for the underdog, they depicted the South African problem as the school bully beating up the weakest boy in the school, and they made no secret of their delight when the Boer settlers were so successful against the might of the British army. Several European counties, like France and Italy, joined Germany in supporting the Boers, and delighted in twisting the lion's tail.

When Edward VII came at last to the throne, Britain was a much detested nation. Also it has to be said that the British Empire and its mother country were looking decidedly frayed at the edges. World trade could no longer be taken for granted, because other countries like Germany and the U.S.A. were rapidly making up lost ground. The British army, still adopting the tactics of the Crimean War, was out of date and led by generals who should have been pensioned off long ago. Its equipment was also obsolete, and its development of machine guns, for example, lagged behind other countries. It's much vaunted navy needed dozens of new and up to date warships if it was to have any claim to rule the waves. Just sitting around singing "Rule Britannia" very loudly carried no weight in a world where sea power depended on ever more powerful and accurate guns mounted on faster and better armoured ships.

A Vauxhall Car

At home the new King faced a challenge with his government. His mother had in her later years been content to sign the papers put in front of her, and only really stir herself when her troops were defeated by the Boers. Edward, with a remarkable vigour and much experience, was determined to make a difference in the world on his country's behalf.

He started off badly with the Prime Minister Arthur Balfour and Foreign Secretary Lord Landsdowne over the visit of the Shah of Persia to Britain. In Persia there had been vicious persecution of Christians, and yet the government had promised the Shah that the King would bestow the Order of the Garter on him. The King refused, but after a standoff he was forced to climb down, and the order was dispatched to Tehran.

14

The King then had a bright idea, and declared he was going on a short cruise, calling in to visit the country of his friend, Soveral, the Ambassador from Portugal. From there the King cruised to Gibraltar, where he was given a great welcome, and to Malta where he was given an even more enthusiastic one. From there it was a short crossing to Naples and Italy, where he was welcomed by Italy's new young King. The visit was hugely successful, with massed crowds full of a warm welcome. In the Kings entourage was a junior member of the government, sent to keep an eye on him and report back. The ministers in London could hardly believe what they were hearing. They were horrified even more when through their spy the King asked for permission to drop in to Paris on his way home by train across France.

By the time Balfour and Landsdowne had signified their refusal to give permission, it was too late. The King's royal train was half way to Paris! Paris was not in any mood to welcome Edward, and still showed much sympathy towards the Boers. But the King showed such trust and friendship towards the French people, and especially the attractive ladies, that he soon won them over. His visit became a triumph of personal diplomacy, and the "Entente Cordiale" became a reality.

Back in London, the government could not overlook the King's great success, however much they would like to do so. The new situation was soon put to the test, when a mob of Serbian anarchists broke into the royal palace in Belgrade, murdered their king and queen and threw their bodies out of a window. They established a new "monarchy" and certain countries like Russia, traditional allies, recognised the new regime after a brief interval. The British government of Balfour wished to follow suit, and to appoint an ambassador to Serbia. King Edward utterly refused.

"One does not throw Kings out of windows" he declared.

The government backed down and the ambassador was never appointed. The opinion of the king was something now to be taken note of, and especially in matters of foreign affairs. His influence continued throughout Europe and beyond until his death in 1910, but the burden placed a great strain on his health. So did the huge number of cigars and cigarettes that he persisted in smoking. But his people rejoiced in a king they could be proud of, a man who unlike his mother went out to be seen and meet people, who was hugely enthusiastic over sports like sailing and horse racing, and if he was perhaps one for the ladies they were happy to overlook that while marvelling at his virility at his age.

Meanwhile there continued to be two Britains. One was the agricultural land, with its well established class system, and its great houses and estates. Here the old established Aristocracy ruled, as many families had done for centuries. And both within the houses and on the surrounding estates, there was a well-recognised hierarchy of servants, which everyone recognised and most accepted. There were a very few cases where a lady of the house ran away with the gamekeeper or the chauffeur, and those on both sides of the green baize doors thoroughly disapproved of such goings on for the most part.

The country was covered in farms, from the large tenant farms on the big estates to much smaller farms owned by a farmer who had been able to buy his land, and then the smaller hill farms in places like Dartmoor and upland Wales, where it was very hard to scrape a living from a small patch of land.

Here, as in other places, the real ruler was the heavy horse. Suffolk Punch, Clydesdale, Percheron, and many others provided the essential motive power (*See frontispiece*). Horsemen lovingly cared for them, and when their working life was over many were "retired" to a quiet corner of the farm. In industry also the horses made a vital contribution, even after the coming of steam, as pit ponies, dray horses, shunting trucks, and in many other ways. In the cities and towns, and in the shires there were other changes. The spread of industry, and the expansion of the railway network had made their mark. The ordinary people could now travel in a way unthinkable eighty years ago. The seaside, and the mountains, moors and dales were within easy reach, and a whole tourist industry got rapidly under way. The seaside landlady became an easily recognised character on the holiday scene, - often the source of a lot of humour!

Beach scene at Swanage about 1900

Meanwhile the social class system of Great Britain trundled along as it had done for centuries. Everyone knew their place, and as far as we can understand most people were contented that it should be so. Old films like "The Admirable Crichton" indicate not only how it was, but point out some of the incongruity of the situation. Dramas like "The Remains of the Day" and "Downton Abbey" give us a clear picture of the social structure of the great houses, and of the regime that existed both above and below stairs.

Steam on road and rail. Witham station in 1910

So the actual Edwardian Era came to an end, and in 1910 Edward VII was replaced by his son, George V. George, unlike his father, had very high moral standards, and his life was closely linked to that of his formidable Queen, Mary. Happiest in his study at Sandringham, sorting out his stamp collection, he was perhaps not really the King Britain needed in the fateful years 1910 to 1914.

The British had not forgotten the near disastrous experience of the Boer War, and the consequent disfavour in which the nation was held by the countries of Europe, - a disfavour which was openly exploited by Germany and her Kaiser. Nor did the Americans look on Britain as a genuine ally. The "jingoism" of the turn of the century was all forgotten, and countries like Austria, Serbia and Russia seemed a long way away. Moreover Britain was looking forward to an even more prosperous future as she traded with the Empire and the world.

Britain's Army was remarkably small, and in many departments out of date. But the British had always been a seafaring nation, and they looked to a strong modern Royal Navy to not only be their means of defence against any enemy, but also to be the means of enforcing British rule and influence wherever it was needed in the world. The oft repeated suggestion "Just send in a gun boat" was regarded as the solution to any international problems, especially in the more remote regions of the Empire.

In the days of Edward VII, who was a great seafarer himself, Admiral Jacky Fisher had been First Lord of the Admiralty, and it was he who inspired the building of the "Dreadnoughts"- the ultimate battleships, which made every other warship afloat obsolete at a stroke. Only a very few countries like Germany, which built their own versions, posed any threat to British sea power. Even the British public became firm supporters of the huge expenditure required to furnish the Navy with these modern ships.

In this period the Balkan States came to be a constant situation of argument and strife, rather as the Middle East has come to be in our own time. The smaller Balkan States, which contained disruptive radical parties and movements, each looked to a larger neighbour to be their patron and protector. So it came about that the Serbians linked up with Russia, in the face of Austria which was an ally of Germany. In all these squabbles, up to 1914, Britain and France stood aloof, but kept a close eye on what was developing.

19

Meanwhile Britain continued to enjoy a considerable degree of peace and political and social stability. There were problems across the water in Ireland, which threatened to spill over into mainland Britain from time to time. The suffragettes became ever more militant, smashing windows and holding marches, with Emily Davidson being killed when she threw herself in front of the King's horse at Epsom. Indeed there were party political swings in the period 1906 – 1914, and Lloyd Georges "Peoples Budget" but by and large Britain, having entered into an "Entente Cordiale" with the old enemy across the Channel, as a result of King Edward VIIs diplomacy, could look across the water, patrolled by her magnificent Dreadnoughts, and could feel that the upheavals in Europe could be watched with interest and otherwise ignored.

Country life Connemara 1909, note lack of shoes

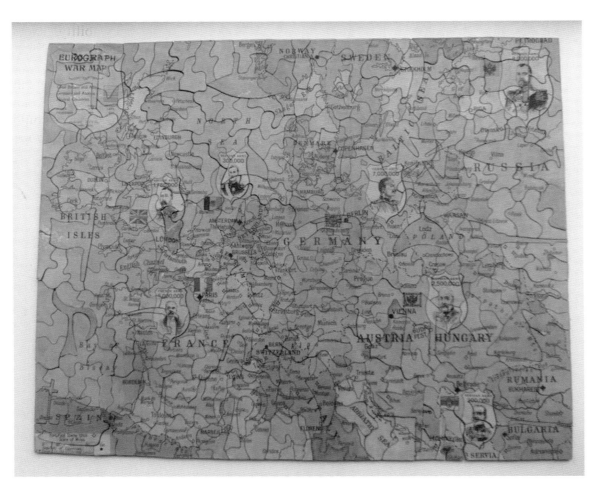

Tuck jigsaw puzzle war map c1914 showing size of European Armies

CHAPTER TWO. THE CALL TO ARMS.

 When on June 28th 1914, a Bosnian Serb anarchist took the opportunity to shoot and kill Archduke Franz Ferdinand, the heir to the throne of the Austro-Hungarian Empire, it at first seemed yet another of those far off events which typified the Balkan states and their chaotic political activities. Over the next 37 days the countries of Europe drifted inexorably into war.

There is no real point in apportioning blame. In the case of Britain, which most concerns us, we had a treaty with Belgium guaranteeing to support that small countries neutrality against any aggressor. The only possible aggressor could be Germany, and the Germans were by that time living in a world of their own. Moltke, a leading German military commander, suggested that Britain had planned the war all along, and he wondered if the Americans could be persuaded to enter the war as Germany's allies if the Germans promised them Canada in return!

The first British Dreadnought battleship and young troops in training c1914

When Edward Grey, the British Foreign Secretary, spoke in the House of Commons on Monday 3rd August, declaring Britain's support for Belgium, he found that the government of Herbert Asquith had the total support of almost every member of parliament, including Lloyd George. As a result the Germans were sent an ultimatum. Germany also declared war on France, with whom we had a treaty. Thus on Tuesday 4th August 1914 the central countries of Europe found themselves engaged in a war which few wanted in their hearts, and for which most were very unprepared.

Von Schlieffen was Chief of the German General Staff from 1891 to 1906. He drew up a secret plan to invade and overwhelm France in 6 weeks. The plan involved two huge German armies invading through Belgium and engulfing Paris in a pincer movement. The neutrality of Belgium was of no account at all. Later the Germans were to argue that their invasion of Belgium was fully justified by the threat from France. (Hitler said much the same about Poland in 1939.) Moltke did not have the same vision and commitment as von Schlieffen and significantly reduced the size of the invading German armies.

The response of the French and British forces was actually pretty chaotic. The Paris garrison and all other troops who could be rounded up sallied forth to meet the Germans, together with the small British Expeditionary Force, and got between the invaders and Paris. On the river Marne the "Miracle of the Marne" occurred, and the invaders were pushed back eastwards to the Aisne, and beyond, and the ghastly static warfare of the trenches developed, from the Channel to the Swiss border.

What was the reaction to all this in Britain? First it should be remembered that Britain had not been involved in any major European war since Waterloo a hundred years before. Second, the nation was still smarting over the events and aftermath of the Boer War. Third, Britain had a strong military tradition. For all young men a career in the Armed Forces, if they were physically fit, was an option. The names of famous regiments were

B-Type London busses were used to transport troops in France throughout the war

known to most people, and songs like "The British Grenadiers" were widely sung. The sound of a military band leading marching soldiers down the street would bring people to their windows and doors.

There was a widely accepted view that the Kaiser was a bully, together with his militaristic Prussian soldiery, despite him being Queen Victoria's grandson. And if bullies like Germany were allowed to get away with trampling all over a little country like inoffensive Belgium, then where would it end? Parliament gave a clear lead, and the country followed with a remarkable degree of unity. And anyway, people reassured one another, a few weeks would settle it, it would all be over by Christmas, wouldn't it? Their sons and brothers would be back in time for the turkey and pudding.

Shooting at Bisley watched by Field Marshal Robert's 1906

…Perhaps it all tickled the spirit of adventure which is present in a majority of young men? What an exciting undertaking to be a part of. What stories to tell the folks round the fire, or down the pub when you got home. It had been a good summer, the harvest was mainly gathered in. It seemed a good time to go and do a spot of campaigning across the water, and see a bit more of the world. Pals and neighbours could join up together, so you would be with your friends, some of them people you had known most of your life.

So, often with great enthusiasm, the younger men of the nation went down to the nearest recruiting office and joined up with Kitcheners army, or Jacky Fisher's Navy. In those weeks which followed August 4th there seems to have been a mild national hysteria. It was actually not necessary for callous and ignorant woman to go round dishing out white feathers. The white feather, when found in the plumage of a black bird was thought to denote some weakness or inferiority, hence the malicious idea of presenting a white feather to a man who was not in the army, suggesting cowardice. The irony of it was that many of these ignorant women not only came to realise in due course the true horrors of such a war, but also discovered that their future husbands, if they should ever

Gresham School Shooting 8 1906, with Guy, Oliver & Roland Tyler.

attract one, were lying buried in a Flanders field. I remember also those women who sadly were never able to marry and have a family because of the consequences of the war.

In England, where the recruits were gathered together and trained, there were reasonable barracks and other requisitioned accommodation, as good food as most of the men were accustomed to, and regular pay, which while not a fortune kept them in the necessities of life. The men quickly developed a great camaraderie, and in the months and years to come this was perhaps the greatest feature of their lives, when all around them was one ghastly unending horror. It was very rare for two men to join up and fight together throughout the four years of war, and to come through alive at the end, but it did happen.

There was another factor at work which very much affected recruiting. The invasion and "rape" of Belgium may have been a starting point, but the Germans did themselves no favours in the following months and years, using poison gas, executing nurse Cavell, arming dummy ambulances and the like. How much of what was broadcast was just propaganda, and how much was true we cannot disentangle a hundred years later, but it stirred up many a young man to sign on and go and seek revenge for atrocities perpetrated by the enemy. Even more did family members join up to avenge the deaths of their loved ones.

Meanwhile the young women of Britain did their share, taking over the jobs of absent men, as farm labourers and factory workers, and especially doing the vile job of manufacturing munitions.

The social class tradition of the country had its direct effect when it came to recruiting. The "lower classes" would be recruited as ordinary soldiers, moved into the infantry regiments, and would have the opportunity to earn a stripe or two, or even three if they soldiered well and kept their noses clean.

Nurse Cavell, executed by the Germans during the war.

The gentry and "upper classes" would provide the officers- many would have been members of Cadet Forces at school or university, and they would be automatically guided to Sandhurst or other officer training schools, and from there they would go to different branches of the army. Those with engineering skills and experience would find themselves in the Royal Engineers, for example.

Just as the new recruits fell for the enthusiastic patter of the recruiting sergeant, so their families really had no idea at all what their young men were letting themselves in for. Nobody did. It was a source of pride that their children, families and friends demonstrated this patriotism. A family member would come back from work and sit down at the tea table.

"You'll never guess what happened today, mum."

"What was that then, dear?"

"You know Fred Jackson, who works opposite me in the factory. Well, last night he went from work down to see the recruiting sergeant, and signed on. This morning he wasn't at work, and the foreman was pretty peeved about it, and threatening to report him, and then this afternoon he breezed in wearing a uniform of the Glumpshire Regiment, and very cocky indeed. We was all struck all of a heap!"

"Has it made a difference to you, dear?"

"Well it certainly makes you think. I don't really know what I ought to do"

All over the land families pondered this question, while peer pressure mounted. It was declared that the jobs of those who enlisted would be waiting for them when the war ended, and they would be welcomed back as victorious soldiers to a land fit for heroes. And, as everyone knew, it would all be over by Christmas.

Among others, two factors affected those young men who considered joining the colours. First of course, was age. The six men we are to consider were born between 1888 and 1899, so that their ages varied from 26 to 15 when war was declared. Some men of course were considerably older. The younger ones, often still at school, worried greatly that the war would not last long enough for them to join up and have their turn. In the event they need not have worried, for it was by no means all over by Christmas 1914!

The second important factor was physical fitness. In the early months, and remembering that it would be a short war, the armed forces were quite selective about who was rated fit to join up. Problems like bad chests and flat feet were causes for rejection. Each man had a fairly comprehensive medical inspection, and we are fortunate to have the results on a form for one of our six men. The training which followed was designed to be tough, for important and obvious reasons. This would also help to weed out those who were not physically and mentally strong enough to survive. At least those responsible for selection and training had a more realistic idea as to what their soldiers would be called upon to face.

So the war, which President Theodore Roosevelt, watching in horror from the far side of the Atlantic, described as "that great black tornado" broke over Europe, and like a real tornado it sucked up all in its path, and particularly in every participating country the young men who should have been that country's future.

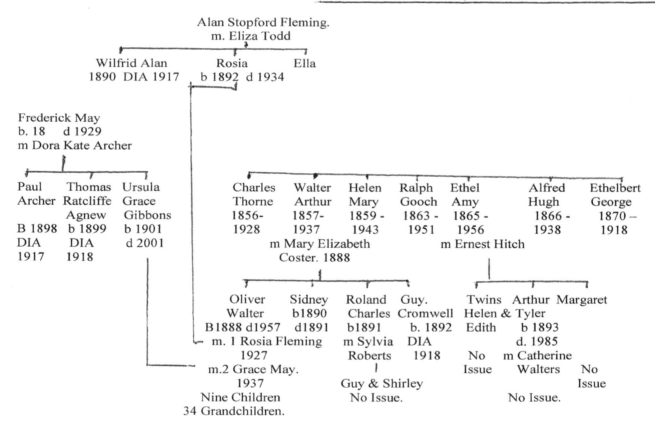

Alan Stopford Fleming.
m. Eliza Todd

Wilfrid Alan   Rosia   Ella
1890 DIA 1917   b 1892 d 1934

Frederick May
b. 18   d 1929
m Dora Kate Archer

Paul   Thomas   Ursula
Archer   Ratcliffe   Grace
            Agnew   Gibbons
B 1898   b 1899   b 1901
DIA   DIA   d 2001
1917   1918

Charles   Walter   Helen   Ralph   Ethel   Alfred   Ethelbert
Thorne   Arthur   Mary   Gooch   Amy   Hugh   George
1856-   1857-   1859 - 1863 -   1865 -   1866 -   1870 –
1928   1937   1943   1951   1956   1938   1918
          m Mary Elizabeth   m Ernest Hitch
          Coster. 1888

Oliver   Sidney   Roland   Guy.   Twins Arthur Margaret
Walter   b1890   Charles   Cromwell   Helen & Tyler
B1888 d1957 d1891   b1891   b. 1892   Edith   b 1893
m. 1 Rosia Fleming   m Sylvia   DIA   d. 1985
     1927   Roberts   1918   No   m Catherine
m.2 Grace May.   Issue   Walters   No
     1937   Guy & Shirley   Issue
Nine Children   No Issue.   No Issue.
34 Grandchildren.

30

CHAPTER THREE. THE MAY FAMILY OF CARDYNHAM.

Rev F G May and his wife Kate

Frederick May was appointed to be the Rector of Cardynham in 1900. The parish lies on the western edge of Bodmin Moor in Cornwall, and consisted of a small group of cottages surrounding the impressive old church, and large Rectory on the hill, and a considerable number of scattered farms, the largest having only 180 acres, and many not much more than smallholdings.

Frederick was 43 when they moved to Cardynham, and Dora Kate, whom he had married in 1896, was two years older than himself. They proceeded to have three children, Paul, born in 1898, Thomas born in 1899, and Ursula Grace, born in 1901. By the time Grace was born her mother was about 50, which was quite remarkable, but not without precedent in the family. The family had very little money, as it was a relatively poor living, and out of his Stipend Fred had to pay for some repairs each year, and also make over a contribution to the pensions of former incumbents of the parish who were now retired. However, Frederick was one of six brothers, several of them quite eminent and successful men, and they received much help from family and friends. The people of the parish were also extremely generous and supportive, and many a gift in kind was left on the doorstep, or pressed into the Rectors hand when he was visiting his parishioners, something he did very conscientiously, and which was much appreciated.

Cardynham Rectory in about 1914

Despite money being very tight, the family always employed three maids, - young girls hoping to be trained for domestic service, anyway until a husband showed up, Outside there was Old Doney, who was the gardener and looked after any livestock, and other helpers from time to time. For transport there was the donkey cart, pulled by bad tempered Kirby, and a pony and trap could usually be borrowed for longer journeys. The railway, organised by Brunel, now stretched from Paddington to Penzance, and Bodmin Road station, on the main line, was not so far from Cardinham.

Cardynham Church

The three children were educated at the Rectory to start with, and even when they were sent away to school, it was an idyllic childhood, vividly remembered later by Grace. They had the opportunity to roam over a lovely area of countryside, with streams, hills and woods, and every variety of natural history. They did a lot of birds nesting, but the rule was you only took one egg from a nest, unless the bird was a predator on other birds. In this way they built up small collections of birds eggs. If a tree was too slender and weak for the heavier boys to climb, Grace was bidden to tuck her skirt into her knickers and climb up, something she delighted in doing as she had the reputation of being a regular tomboy!

Involvement with the church meant usually two Sunday services, and Sunday School, but girls did not sing in the choir. We have no record of Paul and Tom being either bell ringers or choir members. However the rectory children participated in the annual choir tea, and probably in the Choir outing when each year a wagonette and four horses were hired, and everyone went to Looe on the south coast for the day. It was a very merry affair.

Bodmin was five miles away, and was pretty well a full days outing, so the folk at Cardinham learned to fend pretty much for themselves. Mr Wilton was the blacksmith, but he would also turn his hand to a bit of veterinary activity as well. He even branched out into dentistry. On one occasion a visitor at the Rectory was suddenly afflicted with toothache, and was persuaded to go at once to see Mr Wilton. He later described how he was laid flat on his back on the front lawn, and how Mrs Wilton, who was a diminutive lady, sat on his head. The son and daughter, who were heavyweights like their father, then each took an arm. The blacksmith then sat on his chest, and with an old pair of pliers used for horse shoe nails, wrenched out the afflicted tooth! The story may have been a bit exaggerated by the patient when he had reeled back to his expectant audience at the Rectory, but it has the ring of truth, so he must be forgiven!

Three scenes at Cardynham Rectory pre-1910 with Paul, Tom and Grace May and Kirby the Donkey.

Frederick and his brothers had all been educated for most of their schooling by three remarkable spinster aunts, and education was given the highest priority. Paul was sent first to a school at Woolborough, near Newton Abbot in South Devon, and then on to Marlborough College, where the fees were paid for by the wider family.

*Paul, Tom and Grace
May 1906*

*Paul & Tom May,
Cardynham c1910*

In due course Thomas followed in his father's footsteps and went to Sherborne School, which was a little nearer, but both boys faced considerable train journeys at the start and end of each term with changing trains at places like Exeter. Just before the war started Grace was sent to Godolphin School, at Salisbury, a prestigious girls school, with the not inconsiderable school fees being paid by her kind and generous godmother. Again a considerable train journey was involved, but she was at least just up the railway from Thomas, - usually by now called Tom for short.

We have many letters written during this period from the three children to their parents, and also to one another, and these reveal very busy schooldays, with a lot of successes, and also great expectations of lively holiday activities when the terms finished.

Back in Cardynham before the outbreak of the war little had changed, and this state of affairs was welcomed by the whole family, who seem to have been very happy with their situation, even if it involved a lot of hard work. Being sent away to boarding school gave the three a lot of self-confidence, and the ability to travel and be quite independent when necessary. Sending the children

Tom May at the oars, c 1916.

away to school also greatly broadened their outlook. Tucked away in rural Cornwall it was easy to let the world go by, and very tempting to do so, when there was so much enjoyment to be had on the doorstep, as long as one didn't need to have a tooth extracted! But at their schools they mixed with children from all over the British Isles, and they could not avoid learning of world events, as well as the wider news of their own country and its government. When in June 1914 shots rang out in Sarajevo, the children could not be unaware of the growing importance of events which followed.

In addition to this fact, both Marlborough College and Sherborne School had strong military traditions, and ran an Officer Training Corps (Later Combined Cadet Force) which all boys had to join for the duration of their time at school. In these Corps the boys learned military drill, map reading, practical manoeuvres, and other army training, and would do at least one afternoon a week in uniform, supervised by staff members who had been in the military. It was always accepted that for those not up to the academic standard needed for University entrance a career in one of the services would be a very honourable alternative.

Rev. F.G.May, Paul and Tom May

May Family group on parade at Easter 1914, probably at Trelaske House.

By 1914 Fred was about 57 years of age, but still extremely fit physically, and greatly beloved of his parishioners. Why he never sought to make a move is unclear, but he was probably one of the many clergy with a great dedication to his flock, and no desire to lobby his bishop for preferment. The diocese of Truro at that time had a reputation for taking things rather easily. Fred and Kate were hugely aware of the blessing of their three healthy children, granted to them when they were getting on in age. With the support of generous family members and friends they had managed financially down the years, and they could look forward to the days when their children would be launched into the world, empowered with a good education and lots of friends far and wide.

In 1914 Paul, the eldest, was 16, and Tom was 15. Grace was still only 13, and starting at Godolphin. None of the children was anything like old enough to join the armed forces, and even if, as looked more and more likely, war was to break out, everyone predicted a short war, over by Christmas, so the children would not be affected at all. At their schools Paul and Tom watched as the most senior boys, and those who had recently left school, donned smart uniforms and reappeared to show off to the younger ones. There was a good deal of envy for those who would perhaps soon be taking part in a glorious campaign which would be ranked among the great military achievements of the past. Both Paul and Tom reckoned up the months and years and ruefully came to the conclusion that they would themselves never get such a chance.

CHAPTER 4. THE TYLER FAMILY OF HODDESDON.

Hoddesdon High Street in 1890 with Tyler family house at right.

Lil Tyler with pigs at Wormley

In the 1880s Hoddesdon was a large village on the north side of London, astride the Great North Road and connected to London by a very good railway service, so making it a desirable place for those who worked in London to reside. Walter Tyler married Mary Elizabeth Coster in 1888, and they moved to live in a fairly large house in Hoddesdon High Street. The house fronted onto the pavement, but had a spacious back garden.

Walter was the second of seven children, and he ran a wine importing business in the City of London. He is reputed to have pioneered the idea of blending a special wine to be used by churches for Communion services. Oliver, the eldest son, was born in December 1888, so was probably a honeymoon baby. Sidney, who followed in 1889, sadly lived for only a year. Roland was born in 1891, and lastly Guy in 1893.

At this point Walter decided to move his family to what was a small hamlet to the south of Hoddesdon, called Wormley, and here they had a much larger garden, even perhaps a smallholding, where Lil, as Elizabeth was called, could keep some poultry, two dogs, a cockatoo and even a couple of pigs.

Walter & Lil Tyler.

Tyler Boys.

It must have been a lovely place to grow up, and the boys obviously made good use of the garden as well as the house. Each boy was able to have his own bedroom. Already they showed military inclinations, each having a soldiers uniform of late 19th century design, and a broomstick to drill with. They also made a stuffed effigy of President Kruger, as a reminder of the recent Boer War!

Lil was one of three children, and her brother Vincent, known as Vin, decided to emigrate to New Zealand in about 1906. Unfortunately when they got to Vancouver all their luggage was stolen and never recovered, so that they had to trek up onto the Robin ranges near Kamloops, build a log cabin, and remain in Canada, where their extensive family have lived ever since.

Oliver, Guy & Roland Tyler.

Oliver was the first to go to Gresham's School at Holt, in Norfolk, probably in 1902, when he was still 13. The new headmaster, Mr Howson, had great plans for the school, and while the boys were there it moved to a new and spacious site on the east side of the town, near the railway station, where it is still now located. It must have been quite

Guy, Roland & Oliver plus dog.

Guy, Roland and Oliver play Soldiers, a foretaste of things to come.

a rail journey for Oliver, up to London, and then Ipswich, Norwich, and round to Sheringham and Holt.

Fortunately for succeeding generations Oliver kept a diary while at the school, which he also illustrated, and it contains much information seasoned with a lot of humour. The cartoon of the boys dragging themselves reluctantly to the main door of the school, over which is written "Abandon hope, all ye who enter here!" is a classic. All of the three brothers apparently had cameras and were keen photographers, with a very good eye for a picture, and their three photo albums give a wonderful flavour of school life at Gresham's, and both diaries and albums have been of great interest to those at the school today. Roland's album only turned up in late 2015 and has been a priceless addition to the family archive.
Holidays played an important part in the family annual programme, and again the photographs give us an excellent record. The first are dated 1895, when Oliver was about seven, and show the three boys playing on Felixstowe beach. Guy still has to wear a smock, but the older boys are in shorts, and topped off with tam-o-shanters to guard against sunburn! In a year or so the family changed to Swanage in Dorset, further afield but a favourite holiday place for many years.

Pictures from Oliver's diaries at Gresham's School 1906

Guy, Oliver & Roland Tyler on Felixstowe beach, summer 1895.

At Gresham's the boys engaged in a number of sports, shooting, swimming, rugby, cross country, hockey, gymnastics and boxing. They also rowed on the river Lea in the holidays, being enthusiastic members of the Broxbourne Rowing Club. At school they also achieved an unusual distinction as all three of the boys were members of the school Shooting VIII at the same time, as a couple of photographs testify. Oliver in particular continued to be an excellent rifle shot all his life, and did some big game hunting when he later lived in Kenya.

The boys went with the school VIII to take part in competitions at the Bisley range in Surrey, and there are some most interesting photographs of their adventures.

Broxbourne Rowing Club c1910

Walter and his sons on a shooting holiday on Anglesey in 1912.

All the boys participated with enthusiasm in the school Army Corps, and in particular the rifle shooting. Oliver tried to practice every day, - there seems to have been no shortage of ammunition. He was especially pleased when the Corps was issued with new more up to date rifles. On 1st December 1906 Oliver accompanied other army units to Sandringham House, over in west Norfolk,

Guy Tyler aged ten.

and they all lined the field by the grandstand. He saw the King, Edward VII, and Queen Alexandra, and also the Princess of Wales and her three children. (The future Queen Mary, and Kings Edward VIII and George VI.) Oliver's diary records "In the evening we had a school Mission meeting. Must put a D (Penny) in the plate tomorrow." Later on Sunday he notes "did put a penny in the plate, but it had a hole in it" (The penny, not the plate. I don't think that will have done the Missionaries a lot of good!) On the subject of the school diet, he records "Had a good bit of beef for dinner, - a change after a weeks carcass a la gee-gee." Oliver's French was obviously making progress after a slow start!

Tyler family picnic beside the river Lea, Oliver at right. C 1914.

Family holidays began to be more adventurous, with Walter taking the three boys on shooting and fishing trips to Anglesey and to western Ireland, probably Connemara. In Ireland they stayed with a crofter's family in a small cottage, and there are photographs of the family, who are obviously not accustomed to "watch the birdie!" One story from an Irish trip records that the

Boating on holiday in Ireland C 1908.

housewife kept a large stew pot on the go, into which anything they shot was put, once it had been undressed. When the stew pot was not in use, it was pushed underneath the sleeping platform at the far side of the living room. That was all fine, except that at intervals the house dogs could be observed slinking out from under the platform, and licking their lips as they melted away!

One of the mysteries of this happy period is the state of Walter's finances. There seems to have been plenty of money for holidays - albeit not necessarily expensive ones - and for the upkeep of the house in Wormley. They had moved to "The Harpes" in March 1907, according to Oliver's diary. But although Oliver stayed on at Greshams School until he was past 18, in 1907, his younger brothers were withdrawn from the school when they were considerably younger. One can only surmise that the wine business did not earn enough for the continuing school fees. This was hard on both brothers who were academically ahead of their older brother, and who might have won places at university if they had been able to stay longer at school.

Apart from school fees and other expenses, there seems to have been no opportunity for any of the three brothers to join their father in the family firm, and so it was necessary for them to go out and earn a living to support themselves. Oliver, whose abilities were more on a practical level, determined to become an engineer. He obtained an apprenticeship with John Kirkaldy Ltd, of 101 Leadenhall St. E.C.1, and with works at Harlow, who made Refrigerating and ice making machinery, Distilling, Evaporating and Heating Plants. Oliver served a three year apprenticeship with this company until September 1910, taking the exams for the Institution of Civil Engineers, which he passed. During his apprenticeship Oliver worked in all departments of the company, and received an excellent report. He stayed on with the company until the end of 1911.

Oliver Tyler engineer apprentice in c1908.

In early 1912 Oliver moved to work at the Cooperage owned by David Roberts in Tottenham, - the link being that David was a first cousin of the Tylers. Here Oliver was engaged in supervising the machinery at the works, and in the 1950s there was a machine working to cut the grooves for the top and bottom of each barrel, which Oliver had designed and built in the period when he worked there. Tottenham was not that far from Wormley, so Oliver could have commuted to work, or stayed with his cousins at the rather grandly named "Cavendish House" in Tottenham High Road.

Roland also left Gresham's School in 1908, and joined a firm in the City of London, which traded with India in particular, importing tea among other things. He was later described in the school register as an "India Merchant." Eventually he was sent out to work in Calcutta in 1912. This must have been a considerable challenge for him, but he seems to have done well, and he also joined the Indian Army as a "territorial" and appears to have served in the Punjab Volunteer Rifle Battalion, with the rank of Lieutenant.

Roly Tyler in India on Motorbike c1913

Guy had entered Gresham's in 1906, at the age of 14, and left in July 1909 when he was 17, and already a House Captain and school prefect. The school register records that he then went into business in London, like his two brothers, but it doesn't record what that business was, and there seems to be no other information about it. It probably meant that Guy continued to be "home based" to his mother's joy. The three brothers were all very enthusiastic members of the Broxbourne Rowing Club, based nearby on the river Lea. The club had

Roland at work in India.

Topsy Hitch watches Oliver, Roly and Guy raft building.

a very splendid Club house, and organised a lot of social events. One relative, Olive Tyler, remembered lively dances, and that the Tyler boys were much in demand among the local young ladies. Guy stroked the clubs Fours Boat, and also acted as Cox on occasions, which must have been quite a tribute for a stroke needs to be big and strong, and a Cox quite small!

We have quite a number of photographs of this period, probably taken by Oliver and Guy, as they are in albums put together by these two brothers. Roland's album contains a few shared photographs, but does not add much to our knowledge of this period. In 1910 the family returned to their beloved Swanage for their summer holiday, and then in 1912 they went to Anglesey, again for various sporting activities, though 'Lil does not seem to have been with them on this occasion. It must have been after this holiday that Roland went out to India.

About this time Olive, 'Lil's sister, moved down to a cottage at Coombe, near Salcombe, in South Devon, and this fact, coupled with David Robert's purchase of the property at Portlemouth, probably influenced the family decision to take their summer holiday at Salcombe in 1913. This led to a life long association with this beautiful town and estuary not only for Oliver and Roland, but also for succeeding generations of their

Oliver sailing at Salcombe 1913.

families. Many local places like Bolt Head, Hope Cove, Slapton sands and Lea, Dartmouth, Kingsbridge, and Totnes were entered on the family map. The whole South Devon area, taking in Dartmoor as well, had so much to offer. Oliver and Roland were both very keen and able sailors of every size of dinghy and yacht, and the Salcombe estuary was the perfect place to keep and sail such boats.

Lil and Walter Tyler at Salcombe, summer 1913

As the year 1914 unfolded, all three young men must have faced the future with certain feelings of doubt. All had strong sporting interests and accomplishments, and all had enjoyed the achievements and camaraderie of their school days at Gresham's. Working in business, whether it be in London or Calcutta, must have been at times fairly soul destroying. None of them could visualise, even after the assassination of Archduke Franz Ferdinand at the end of June 1914, that within a couple of months their lives would be turned upside down.

It seems likely that Oliver offered himself for active service very soon after the outbreak of war on 4th August 1914. He was called before a medical board on August 27th, to assess his fitness for the Special Reserve of Officers. The report signed by Lt. Anderson R.A.M.C. of Millbank Hospital gives all Oliver's vital statistics, - height 5 ft. 8 ½ inches, weight 122 lbs, - less than 9 stone by my reckoning! And he is described as "Fit." which is not surprising, considering all that rowing. Before his medical examination Oliver's former headmaster at Gresham's School had to fill in three forms on his behalf, certifying that he had reached a satisfactory standard of education. Oliver also stated that he could ride a horse, which would become very important.

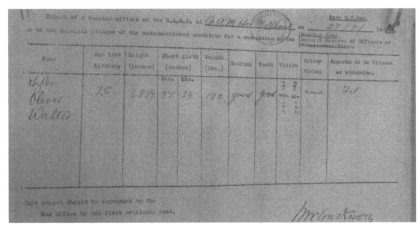

Oliver Tyler medical certificate issued on joining the army in August 1914. He was classed as "Fit."

Oliver was a very valuable recruit for the army given his engineering qualifications and experience, and it is not surprising to find that his commission as a Second Lieutenant, Land Forces, from the King, was signed the day after his medical examination. He was sent at once to the School of Mechanical Engineering, at Chatham, which was a main training school for the Royal Engineers. There he learned his trade as a Field Officer R.E.

In October 1914 Oliver was posted to the 92nd Field Company, R.E. but continued at Chatham. It is probable that because of his skills and experience as an engineer Oliver was kept on at Chatham SME as an instructor, something he would have been very good at. On July 6th 1915, his training completed, he was promoted to Temporary Lieutenant. Presumably this was in recognition of his work as an engineer. On July 28th 1915, nearly a year after the outbreak of war, Oliver went over to France with the 92nd Field Company Royal Engineers, and began his overseas service at Le Havre, moving then by train to Coisy, near Amiens. This area of what became known as the Somme battlefield, stretching from the river Somme in the south and east to the allied trenches was to be Oliver's home territory until mid-1918, and he must have covered many thousands of miles on horseback and come to know almost every inch of it.

Capt. Oliver Tyler in Royal Engineers uniform 1915.

A page from War Diary 0f 92nd Coy R.E. signed by Oliver Tyler in 1916.

A summary of the War Diary of the 92nd Field Company R.E. for August 1915 gives a very clear idea of one of the tasks Oliver would have supervised:

" Generally speaking, from 6.8.15 to 31.8.15. the company has been employed in selecting sites for redoubts, laying them out, and supervising infantry working parties of about 2000 to 3000 men and doing the technical work of revetting and tunnelling, and building bomb proof dug outs with 10 ft. overhead cover. Also casting reinforced concrete slabs for roofs of dug outs."

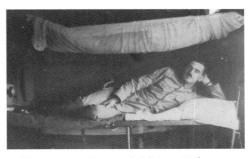

The only photo of Oliver Tyler on active service, - at rest! C 1916.

By Sept. 1st 1915 the Company were billeted at Millencourt, just to the west of the town of Albert, and a few miles north of the river Somme. The engineers continued to supervise the building of trenches and dug outs, and the diary records:

"N.B. Dug outs constructed with floor level 14 feet below ground line,- 6 feet head room, and two feet earth and chalk above ground line. Some dug outs roofed with timber, others with girders and reinforced concrete slabs." Not hard to guess which were the most

"The Innocent abroad" cartoon by Capt. Bruce Bairnsfather.

sought after! The dug out was home for the British Tommy, as Bruce Bairnsfather's wonderful cartoons constantly remind us.

Bruce Bairnsfather again: "There goes our Blinkin parapet again." Cartoons published in the Bystander Magazine during the war and very good for morale!

In September 1915 the 92nd Company marched to new billets at Dernancourt, south of Albert, and nearer both to the river Somme and the front-line trenches to the east. This now became Oliver's theatre of operations, with a dump of Engineer materials in the village of Pozieres on the Albert-Bapaume road. Oliver is mentioned as being in charge of supervising the building of new trenches, and this involved two nights out in the open laying out support trenches, and directing the infantry diggers. Every month a casualty list was attached to the war diary, and that for September 1915 records those who were sick, and also that there was an accident and one driver died. Casualties were quickly replaced with new recruits, but experience lost was hard to replace. Horses were also vital and precious to the work of the sappers, and looked after very carefully.

One of the adverts for "Sunshine Soap" in a 1915 vintage magazine claims that "The British Tommy is the cleanest soldier in the trenches!" Oliver and his men spent a lot of time, according to the diary, laying on water supplies, and building bathing establishments and washrooms. It must have made a nice change from putting up barbed wire at night! The casualty list for October notes that one sapper was accidently wounded through tampering with an unexploded shell. A court of inquiry found one driver and one sapper had been negligent.

In November they made field ovens and laid board walks to try and get out of the mud and water, and there is an excellent diagram of a 6' x 4' dugout, again very akin to Capt. Bairnsfathers sketches. They laid a board wall in Aberdeen Avenue. The names given to all the trenches are most fascinating. They moved a 1600 gallon tank from the front to the back of a chateau, and plugged the bullet holes in it. Rather a necessary task! One of their Lieutenants was evacuated sick to base, and has not re-joined.

Now it is December 1915, and the diary notes "Three days of heavy frost have been followed by heavy rain, - the frost disintegrated the chalk and the trenches have fallen in." There is then a whole page beginning "The experience of the last week shows the absolute necessity of adhering to the rules and principles in Military Engineering for construction of trenches….." Trying to maintain the construction of the trenches in winter conditions must have been a fearful challenge for Oliver and his men. One sapper was killed by the accidental discharge of a rifle being cleaned in a billet.

In January 1916 they were felling timber for their saw mill, - one hopes the French were happy about that! This was to make dugouts, and they were also repairing one of the tramlines, so essential for moving materials through the mud. They ran a pulsometer pump to try and clear the chateau well. In fact the engineers under Oliver and the other officers tackled every conceivable type of task and challenge, often under shell fire. The steam engine for their sawmill at Chipilly broke down, and Oliver had to get a new piston and connecting rod made by an engineer in Amiens. By January 28th they had repaired the engine and the circular saw was in use again. It must have been a very useful tool

A soldier comforts his dying horse. Statue in Chipilly. Photograph in May 2015.

They worked on the standard gauge railway which reached Chipilly, and built a 50 foot long platform, while one section of the company worked at the 3rd Army School over at Flixecourt. Making dugouts continued to be the main task of the company. On February 27th, Oliver, now a Captain, was detached as an instructor at 18 Division school, and Captain Field became Company Commander. In the middle of March the company began to move to Bray and Suzanne, on the river Somme. At the end of the month Oliver and six other ranks were sent again to 18 Div. School for duty at La Houssoire.

The variety of work intensified in April including making "Dog Kennel" dugouts in the fire trenches, - I can imagine what Bruce Bairnsfather would have made of those! On April 12th Oliver and his team returned to the company. They repaired a roof that had been blown off by a shell, but there seem to have been no serious casualties, perhaps because they were engaged behind the trenches a great deal.

They did not know it, but much of their work was preparing supply routes for the coming battle of the Somme. They laid a further 700 yards of the steam hauled narrow gauge railway that we later travelled on, designed to carry supplies up to the front line trenches. Two pages of the diary here are signed by Oliver. One sapper was killed in action during the month.

Two views of the railway built by Oliver Tyler and his troops to carry materials up to the front before the first battle of the Somme. This railway is still running. Photographs taken in 2015 by Tricia Tyler.

On 1st July the battle of the Somme erupted around the company, and a shell knocked out an officer and four sappers. They worked desperately under shell fire to consolidate ground taken from the enemy, and to bring up necessary supplies. At 9.30 p.m. they were working to repair their railway line, - perhaps the one we travelled along nearly a hundred years later! Casualties were suffered all the time because of heavy shelling. The Huns did not like being driven backwards. The diary reveals much work being done under very dangerous conditions, and several times help was given to the Royal Artillery, probably to haul their guns through the mud. By the middle of the month they were doing much work on water supplies and roads, - or what was left of them. In the evening of July 14th Captain Field, the Commanding Officer was killed while supervising the transport of materials. The company was then taken out of the line and sent by train to rest billets at Hocquincourt. July 22nd notes "All sections resting." They must indeed have been exhausted.

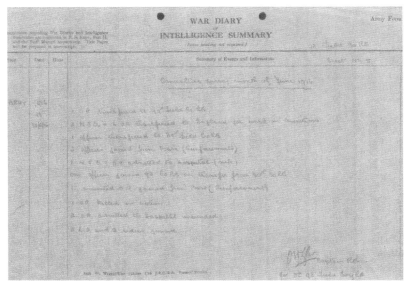

The monthly casualty list in the War Diary, again signed on this occasion by Capt. Oliver Tyler, dated in 1916.

On July 18th the company had marched to Staple, and they were inspected in full marching order by General Morse. Oliver Tyler was confirmed as Commanding Officer of the 92nd Company, and the General Order number is quoted. Casualties for the month were one officer killed and one wounded, and 6 other ranks killed with 26 wounded. It had been a very demanding month for them.

In September Oliver writes to Miss Rosia Fleming and tells her he had five brief days of leave in August, which he spent at Salcombe in S. Devon. Part of his letter is worth quoting:

"I cannot give news, but you can read all about it in the papers. Now that the novelty has worn off, there is not much glamour about the modern show. Just a lot of loud noise and rather unsafe. When you are really at your wits end for amusement, just write down what the moors look like, and your opinion of the crops, and any old thing connected with peace and plenty, and send it to Yours Sincerely, Oliver W. Tyler."

Meanwhile, on the western front there continued to be loud noise and lack of safety, as the battle of the Somme is reckoned to have continued until November, and Oliver was in the thick of it as the Commanding Officer of 92 Field Company R.E. John Glubb, in his war diary "Into Battle" was serving within a few miles of Oliver at this crucial time, and he depicts in graphic detail how conditions became almost intolerable as winter approached with rain, cold and mud, and casualties mounting steadily. The War Diary of the 92nd Company was a sanitised production for the eyes of the Colonel or the General. John Glubbs memoir gives a much truer picture, so that as you wade through glutinous knee deep mud you can smell the rotting corpses left unburied on all sides. That explains graphically the last paragraph of Oliver's letter to Rosia.

Capt. Oliver Tyler (centre) and 1 Section, 92nd Coy R.E. Note bridging pontoon at rear. 1915.

As winter advanced, the diary becomes less easy to read. The exhausted scribes had little time for writing. Men and horses continued to die together. Pumping plants were installed at Thiepval Wood, Blighty Valley and Crucifix corner. Thiepval, today the site of a huge war memorial, was frequently shelled and the pump there had to be withdrawn. On the 4th October, Oliver led number 1, 3 and 4 sections up to dugouts near the redoubt. The rest of the month was spent in support, repairing trenches and dugouts, water supplies and railways. The battle had made a ghastly destruction everywhere, but at least the casualties were far fewer.

November followed the same pattern, and in December someone with minute writing managed to get the whole month onto a single sheet of paper! January continued with much activity, repairing tunnels, huts, dugouts and trenches, and then on January 19th Oliver was transferred to 17 Corps headquarters. On February 16th he was moved to 19 Corps Field Engineers, and on May 28th he was appointed Adjutant. He had been promoted Acting Major on 30th November 1916.

Oliver served as Assistant to the Chief Engineer of 19 Corps until the end of the war, and we lose sight of his day to day activities. However it was obviously not just sitting behind a desk telling other people what to do.

Albert Church destroyed in 1918.

In March 1918, as the Germans made one last great effort to crush the allies, Oliver was awarded the Belgian Croix De Guerre. The citation gives a glimpse of his activities as a soldier

"For consistent good service during the period July 1915 to August 1918, and especially during the retreat on the Somme in March 1918, when the Chief Engineer was severely wounded he helped to carry on the work with untiring energy and conspicuous zeal. His services were of the greatest assistance. On one occasion when explosives were required urgently for

The church in Albert rebuilt now in 2015.

demolitions he collected these, and personally conveyed them under heavy fire to the site of demolition, thereby enabling the bridge to be destroyed in time."

At the end of March 1918, Oliver again wrote to Rosia Fleming, and again his letter is very interesting: "We are having a bit of a battle as you will have gathered from the papers. We are all cheerful and killing plenty of Huns. Thanks awfully for your cheerful letter. I am very sorry to hear that your brother has been killed. There will be fine company in the Halls of Valhalla these days, and none finer than the R.F.C. Contingent." (RFC was Royal Flying Corps, and we shall meet Wilfrid Fleming later on. Rosia did not have a lot to be cheerful about. Oliver

King George V visits his troops "somewhere in France" in the summer of 1918.

was at this stage a rather nominal Unitarian. Hence perhaps the Halls of Valhalla reference!) He continues: "I have just had a night's sleep, the first for a week, 'tho I have taken cap-naps by the road or where I could. I should like to finish it up and do my long promised pilgrimage over the moors. Joan has promised me a card of herself as a bridesmaid. It will be charming I am sure, and a valuable

Capt. Oliver Tyler and dog on leave during the First World War 1916.

addition to my gallery of old friends. I am reserving a space for yours someday when you do not feel too coy." (Could have been put a little more tactfully, perhaps?) " It was kind of you to think of cream, but you must not send food out of England. We are well fed here. I am a Captain only. Best of luck, Yours very sincerely. Oliver W. Tyler."

Oliver had been an acting Major for some time, but the War Office had the very unfair tactic of dishing out acting ranks and then withdrawing them at the earliest opportunity to save money!

It is rather surprising to find that Oliver was not demobbed until April 25th 1919. Why did he have to wait a further five months after the armistice? The reason was that if you have a splendid war for over four years, concentrated on a relatively small area in Eastern France, the mess is indescribable. As soon as the war was over, many relatives of those who had been killed wanted to cross the Channel and fulfil a pilgrimage to the place where their loved ones had died. They wanted to see graves in a cemetery, and read a headstone, or plan one.

The problem was that the whole area was a ghastly mess, and highly unsafe. The Royal Engineers, with their heavy equipment and bomb disposal skills were desperately needed to supervise the thirty thousand Chinese labourers who toiled to do the dangerous clearing up task. Thus Oliver's war went on until April, and it must have been a very frustrating period and a dangerous one, and he must have longed to be home in England.

Oliver had "a good war" as it was glibly described by those who never crossed the Channel. He was not killed or seriously wounded, he received promotion, he was decorated for bravery. One of his two brothers also survived. He learned a very great deal in those four traumatic years. Finally he more or less learned how to cope with personal trauma in his own life. Like virtually

Oliver Tyler record of service for the period 1915 – 1919. The book reappeared after 100 years!

all his comrades in arms, he wiped the whole episode from his memory. He did not talk about or write about it. He had just a half dozen photographs of the whole war period, and these were hidden away. We do not know what happened to his medals. His Record of Service book surfaced in my house, at the back of a drawer, and we do not know how it got there or where it was hidden away for nearly a hundred years.

In the event it has been the work of a researcher here in England which has discovered the War Diary of the 92nd Company of Field Engineers, and has enabled us to put together the jigsaw puzzle of Oliver's involvement in the First World War. It is amazing that all this information has only now surfaced at the moment when we are commemorating the centenary of the war.

As we have seen, Roland, having had to leave school early when he could have expected to stay on and go to University, then went into business in the city of London in 1908, and then sailed for India in 1912, and was

described in the Gresham's School Magazine as an "India Merchant." Roland fitted in apparently well and quickly among the English community in Calcutta. On 4th December 1913 he joined the Indian Army, as a Private in the Calcutta Volunteer Rifles, - it must be remembered that he had been a very good shot with a rifle when at School. War was declared between Great Britain and Germany on August 4th 1914, and for some reason we do not know Roland was transferred to the Royal Engineers on 24th August 1914 with the rank of Sapper. Whether at this time he was still in India, or had returned to England is also not clear. Roland must have been back in England early in 1915, and he

Roland Tyler in Indian Army uniform c 1914.

French maidens try Roland's Dispatch rider's motorbike for size during a friendly meeting.

was duly posted to Flanders on March 10th 1915. He was still seconded to the Royal Engineers and was promoted to the rank of Corporal, with the post of

Dispatch Rider. By the end of September he had taken part in the battles of Neuve Chappelle and Loos.

Dispatch riders meeting to exchange notes, France.

It should be remembered that in the First World War communications played a most important role, and provided endless problems for the signallers. It was soon discovered that the semaphore systems used in training in rural England were not recommended on the battlefields of France. Standing up so that all may see you, and waving a couple of flags aloft was calculated to attract the undivided attention of every enemy sniper in the area.

The signallers, members of the Signals Section of the Royal Engineers, soon adopted the same underground existence as their fellow comrades in arms. They dug deep and well insulated houses along the trenches, and then connected themselves up to the outside world with thin wires, tacked to the sides of the trenches. They then used field telephones to speak to the world, and if the background noise on their busy lines became too overwhelming, they resorted to "Buzzing" their messages in Morse Code. Hence their nickname of The Buzzers. (A wonderful description of their work and challenges is to be found in "Carrying on after the first hundred thousand" by Ian Hay, who served in those trenches through the war, and really knew what he was talking about!)

If the telephone lines were rendered useless by passing shrapnel and the like, there were two other means of communication. Always remembering, of course, that for obvious reasons it was considered most important to prevent the enemy from reading your messages. One of these was the use of carrier pigeons. I do apologise to all bird lovers, but it was felt that a pigeon's life was fairly expendable. If as a result of great bravery or sheer bad luck your bird "did not make it," its body might be retrieved and used as the foundation for a nice little casserole. It would indeed not have died in vain.

The final method of communication was the motor cycle dispatch rider, and this is where Roland Tyler, Corporal R.E. makes his entrance. The family tradition was that as Roland could not afford a horse, upon arrival in France he was issued with a motorcycle, and appointed a dispatch rider. There may have been a little truth in this, but it

The cherished motorbike in action.

seems more likely that Roland, who had all the instincts of an engineer, like his brother Oliver, had a desire to ride motor cycles, and an ability to start them and keep them going which made him ideal for this vocation. And it was truly a vocation. For almost all soldiers on the battlefields of Eastern France, their first encounter with shrapnel, machine guns and snipers convinced them very quickly to get underground as quickly as possible. A well dug trench was not guaranteed to preserve your life, but it was an infinitely better bet than walking around out in the open. Worse still was riding around on a motor bike, providing a tasty target for all Germans with a sporting frame of mind.

Rider and bike take a break.

Thinking about it now, with hindsight, it must be suggested that the front line area, with its systems of tranches, both firing and support, and it's communications trenches, would have been an impossible place to ride a motor cycle around. Further, at night, with the minimum illumination possible, so as not to give your position away, the chances of you charging into somebody's trench would have been very high, and the chances of getting shot by your own friends almost a certainty.

I think that the main reason that Roland survived until July 1917 was because most of his work was in the back areas. Yes, artillery shells might land at any time in any place, but at least a single dispatch rider would not count as worthy of special targeting and the expenditure of a boche shell. In the photographs that have recently come

Malle Claire.

to light, we can see Roland enjoying a wayside halt, much as one would have done on a days outing along the leafy lanes of Rural Hertfordshire. Other more senior officers, with private means, like Lieutenant Glubb would have travelled about on horseback.

It must be remembered that while urgent and brief messages could be sent through field telephones, like the grid reference on an enemy troop concentration needing a bit of shelling, there must also have been a huge quantity of more bulky material such as divisional orders, quartermasters returns, war diaries and the like which would have been ideally transported by a dispatch rider. Roland was attached to the Royal Engineers, who had their workshops and supply dumps in the "back areas", so when his brother Oliver needed urgent spare parts for his sawmill at Chopilly, Roland might well have ridden at speed north to Amiens to get the repairs made.

Incidentally, it is interesting to note that recent discoveries put all three brothers in the same area for part of the war, between 1915 and 1917. Oliver and Guy took no photographs at all, though we know both of them possessed cameras. But Roland took a number of most valuable and interesting photographs. Was this because his job took him quite far afield, and he was a natural photographer? Or did

Roland (left) and bike rest beside the road

both Oliver and Guy find their experience of the war so ghastly that they did not want to record it in any shape or form? We shall never be able to know the full answer to that paradox.

Two French ladies who looked after the Dispatch riders in 1915.

Roland, as a dispatch rider attached to the Royal Engineers, did not feature in a war diary such as his brother Oliver's, and also being a Corporal and not an officer he would not have the responsibility of writing up a diary. However, the

War Diary of the 92nd company Royal Engineers gives us a very good idea of the sort of work he was doing, and where. The dispatch riders must have also been something of an independent outfit, and this is borne out by the photographs we have, showing them meeting up with one another.

The period when Roland was based in the Somme Valley was the climax of the war, with the first Battle of the Somme starting on 1st July 1916, and continuing on until winter. Fighting continued fiercely all along the front through 1917, with perhaps the battle of Cambrai and the use of tanks in force for the first time giving a small indication that the bloody stalemate of trench warfare and "pushes" might be coming to an end.

It is amazing that Roland came through it all unscathed. What his mental state was by July 1917, it is impossible to conjecture. It may be that it was thought best for him to be returned to India in a training role. There can have been relatively few soldiers who were spared from further warfare in France during this period, but Roland could speak Hindustani, and the allies on the

No dispatch rider can resist a good snowball! Winter 1915

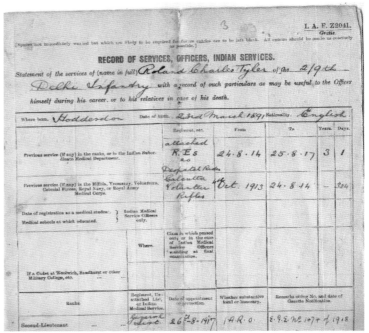

Lt. Roland Tyler record of war service in India and in France 1914 to 1919. This appeared again in 2015.

Western Front were in desperate need of more troops, following the collapse of Russia, and consequent move of huge masses of German troops from the Eastern Front to the West.

One of the interesting documents that has come to light is a letter in Roland's handwriting dated 16th July 1917, and sent to the Military Secretary of the India Office in London. By this time his return to India had been officially approved, though he does not as yet know the intended date of his embarkation. He writes as follows:

"I have the honour to request that I may be granted a month's leave in England before proceeding to India. In support of my application I beg to state that I have spent 34 months on active service in France, and consequently my private affairs are in such a state that they demand my close attention for some weeks. I have the honour to remain your obedient servant, R.C.Tyler."

In August Roland gave his address in England as that of his Aunt Olive, at Woodlands, Salcombe, Devon. I have found an interesting family group photograph in Roland's album. It is dated 1913, and it shows a group, all well clothed, on the sand by rocks beside the Salcombe Estuary. The group consists of David Roberts, his daughter Ella, Mrs Roberts, (in splendid hat) and in front Sylvia Roberts, the older daughter, Roland's wife to be, but not until 1925. It seems likely that the Roberts family might well have been staying down at Ferryside, East Portlemouth, opposite Salcombe, in the summer of 1917 when Roland obtained his months leave in England.

Walter & Lil picnic 1917?

Another of the documents we now have is the Medical Certificate issued following an examination in London and dated June 7th 1917. Roland Tyler's height and weight are recorded as satisfactory, and he is classified as "fit." As a result of this his commission as a 2nd Lt. in the Indian Army Reserve of Officers was approved, and so was his return to India in Autumn 1917.

The War Office in London recorded Roland Tyler as joining the Indian Army Reserve of Officers on November 2nd 1917, which must have been about the time he landed back at Calcutta. The Indian Army records tell us where Roland was posted, but not what his role was, though we know he was rapidly promoted to full Lieutenant. On November 25th Roland was officially attached to the Delhi Infantry, and on December 14th he joined the

Troops in training, India 1918.

Guy on family holiday in 1912.

Regimental Depot of the Regiment which was in Delhi. There he served for a total of 281 days, presumably training soldiers ready for overseas service. His experience of the war in France must have been a huge asset to the training schedule.

Finally, on September 20th 1918 Roland was transferred to the 2/150 Infantry, Indian Army, where he served until he was demobbed on March 3rd 1919. The photographs suggest that he may have continued as a "Territorial" in the Indian Army for a period, but so far no details of this service are known.

Roland Tyler had what would be described – by those who had never been in France, - as a "Good War." He was never wounded as far as we know, at least physically. He achieved creditable promotion, rising through the ranks to the position of Lieutenant. He was awarded the appropriate Medals for the campaigns he was involved in. He must have exhibited conspicuous bravery to scuttle around the battle area as a Dispatch Rider on a very exposed motor cycle. We shall see how his life developed in the next few years in India, and then beyond that back in England.

The youngest of the three brothers, Guy Cromwell Tyler, joined the Artist's Rifles almost immediately after the outbreak of war, and his fortunes in the army as an infantryman were a sharp contrast to those of his two older brothers. Having been in his school Cadet Force, and also been an expert marksman in the school shooting team, he would have had no problem with basic training, and probably outshone a lot of Artists!

By the end of October his training was complete and he travelled with his Regiment to North East France, the scene of much fighting. His brothers would not arrive in France for five and nine months respectively, so Guy had a good start as far as active service was concerned.

His Regiment was involved in the carnage of the First Battle of Ypres, and after this Lord French, the Commander in Chief, offered a number of commissions to the Artists' in the old line regiments of the famous First Seven Divisions, which had suffered such severe losses during the first few months of this war which was to be over by Christmas. Guy Tyler accepted one of these commissions when it was offered to him, and after going through further basic training in France, he was Gazetted to the Norfolk Regiment in January 1915. It is probable that he would have known other soldiers in the 1st Norfolks who had been

The great Cloth Hall in Ypres destroyed in 1916, and now rebuilt splendidly today.

fellow pupils with him at Gresham's School. By this time Guy would have been 22 ½ years old.

Guy obviously valued his old school very highly, and he took the trouble, unlike his brothers, to write letters back to Gresham's for publication in the School Magazine. In February 1915, when he had settled in with the Norfolk Regiment, he wrote: " I was very pleased to get your letter, which was waiting for me at a farm about one mile behind the firing line, when I went back for an hour last night to draw rations and have a hot meal.

Guy Tyler in training.

I am replying from my shelter in the firing line, as I am now in charge of about 50 yards out of the 250 miles of it, and during the day I am glad to say things are slack. We are returning "to rest" tonight, and altogether the time we spend actually "in" now is very small. At the moment, it is four days in the trenches, four days in support

Capt. Guy Tyler in the Norfolk Regt.

billets, and eight days' rest, about four miles back. This time we have struck a dry spell, though with a cold wind at times and slight snow. As you know the trenches have been in a very bad state; however, and improvement in the weather coupled with an energetic system of improvement of earth works, has made a big difference, and this regiment is noted out here for the amount it does to help. As an example, we enter the firing line at, say, 8.p.m.; alternate men are put on watch, and the remainder fill sandbags, rebuild all the front parapet and loopholes, drain the place by a ditch along the back, and build up what protecting banks of sandbags we can. This takes most of the night and keeps the men busy, but these Norfolk men, mostly from Norwich and Yarmouth, are a very good type and really enjoy the work. The officer is supposed to be up all night, so one keeps dozing during the day, until a shot comes with a crack against the sandbags and wakes one up. It is rather like marking on the range behind a somewhat unsafe butt."

(This is a reference to shooting on a practice range at school or Bisley using a .303 rifle in the open air at ranges of 200 – 1000 yards as a rule.)

" It seems to be more or less etiquette here, at the moment, not to do much shelling of each other's trenches, for which we are duly thankful. There is a continuous stream of shells over the top at batteries, farms and villages with a continual bang! Thud! Whistle! Crash!! The little amount of damage done by them is extraordinary, although the fields near their targets are usually dug up with dozens of small duck-pond holes.

The men are very cheerful, and they have spent some time this morning heating a pail of water drawn from a shell hole during the night, and washing and shaving themselves; they take no notice of the trouble it needs to do this. We get hold of a good supply of braziers and coke now, which the men appreciate very much, while another good thing, served out now for wet trenches, is strong rubber top-boots."   G.C.T.

Typical war damage in Bethune still dominating the town in 1921, on market day.

It is interesting that Guy seems to have been able to send home a lot of interesting information, and this for publication in a magazine, but perhaps it was not information which would have been of any use to the enemy, and on the contrary boosted the morale of the British troops. By May 1915 Guy had had a further three months of trench warfare, and he again wrote to the School Magazine:

" We were, as you imagined, in the Hill 60 show, but slightly on a flank, and some of the other regiments did all the heavy work of the charges and counter attacks, though our co-operation foiled the Germans counter moves. We had one officer killed and six wounded, but spread over several days. As you will have seen, one of the regiments always working with us suffered very heavily, the 1st Bedfords. We have now been in the firing line and close support for three weeks, during which time I have, of course, been out of doors all the time, - up in the morning always by 3 o'clock, often not sleeping at night at all, but in the comparative safety of daytime. No bath, and my clothes never off, this is what I feel more than anything.

French cavalry patrolling a road in France in 1914.

The "Artists" men who have taken commissions are naturally suffering very severely, because every single one has gone straight into the firing line, and a great number that I knew, both at home and in the "Artists" afterwards, have been killed. I believe that of the first 50 to go through the School of Instruction with me over half are already casualties.

Bruce Bairnsfather again: "Well, if you knows of a better 'ole, go to it!"

You may not agree with me, but the feeling of all of us here is that the workmen in England should be put under military law just as much as the men out here and shot for desertion if they quit their jobs in the same way, for after all their lot is much easier and their pay much higher than that of soldiers; whilst, if the supply of munitions suddenly gives out, they simply leave the men here to be slaughtered, in just as definite a way as if a sentry goes to sleep on his post." G.C.T.

Strong words, and the bit about casualties very prophetic, for by the time this was published in the magazine Guy was a casualty himself. The definition of a "blighty" is not easy, but in essence it was a wound in action, requiring hospital treatment, and withdrawal from active service, but not causing permanent disablement. For the men at the front a blighty was the only honourable way out. They had signed on to do their bit, and as Guy indicates were cheerful and willing at least in 1915. By 1918 it might be a different story. But if you got a blighty you would be invalided home, and although you would remain on the strength of the army no-one demanded that you should be sent back to the slaughter. There were a lot of safe and honourable jobs to be done in England for those who showed with pride that they had been wounded in action.

Guy was severely wounded towards the end of May, 1915. A photograph of him with his mother only came to light a few months ago. It shows two things. Guy was wounded in the right arm or hand and his arm is bandaged and in a sling. Second, his mother's expression says "My baby has been restored to me, and no way is he going back to risk his life in that terrible war."

Unfortunately for his doting mother, Guy was a man of great courage and devotion to duty. As he made a good recovery, he thought more and more of his comrades facing the horrors of trench warfare, attacks and counter attacks, which he had experienced and knew so well. How could he face them if he just stayed at home using his wound as an excuse, and living a life of safety and comfort? There must have been terrible rows with his mother, but Guy was determined, and in October 1915 he re-joined the Norfolk Regiment with a home posting at their base in Folkestone. It was the first stepping stone to getting back to active service in France.

Guy Tyler, wounded, with his mother, Wormley 1915.

Guy must have realised that he could spend the rest of the war behind a desk in Folkestone, as he was still considered unfit for active service, so he looked around and succeeded in getting himself appointed Adjutant to a battalion of the Northumberland Fusiliers in Newcastle-on-Tyne. Here he would have had an important training role, as well as an administrative one. However, in Autumn 1916, while great battles raged in France, the battalion was disbanded, and Guy was returned to the Norfolk Regiment in Folkestone, albeit now as Adjutant and with the rank of Captain.

In January 1917, while still classified as unfit for active service, Guy volunteered for base work abroad, and was put in charge of a Prisoner of War company in France. It was typical of Guy that he would exchange a desk job in England to get back across the channel, and be nearer the action and his comrades. He wrote an interesting article for the Gresham's School Magazine telling the school all about his new situation and work:

"A Prisoner of War company consists of two English Officers, an escort, and 450 German prisoners of all ranks below officers. The prisoners are kept in the same company as much as possible, and my company has just been celebrating (quel mot) the anniversary of its formation, the greater part having been captured at Courcellette in September 1916. On formation a Company is given one or two German Sergeant Majors, eight Corporals, six interpreters, a certain number of carpenters and other useful men, a few medical men, and the rest labourers. They then have the whole organisation complete, and they can be divided into Platoons and Squads under the NCOs just like a British Company.

Cambrai church still in desolate ruins in 1921.

The bulk of the prisoners work all day road making, railway making, quarrying etc., and are in an extraordinarily fit condition. They get good food, - as good as our own troops,- and have a canteen in their compound supplied by goods from English canteens. They have money sent from Germany, and also receive working pay for all days on which they work. They also have a large supply of parcels from Germany, the most common contents being black bread, tobacco, and cigarettes, though they contain many other things.

Their chief amusements,-besides eating,- are singing and playing on musical instruments, partly homemade, and partly from Germany. The choirs practice with great thoroughness and are very good, while my company has a really brilliant string band. There are some very clever craftsmen amongst them, and, if you are able to turn them on to their own trades, they take a great delight in their work.

Of course we get a lot of jeers for treating them so well, but they are very well behaved and give no trouble at all, and it is not usual with us as a nation to kick a man when he is down. That is what it comes to."   G.C.T.

In the Autumn of 1917 Guy achieved his great desire and re-joined his beloved Norfolk Regiment. His battalion were then sent south to Italy, where Guy was specially commended for work he did surveying and making new maps for use by the army.

The great memorial and cemetery at Thiepval, 2015."

War cemetery Foncquevillers, 2015

In April 1918 his battalion were posted back to France, and Guy was promoted to Captain (again?) and became the Adjutant. This was a period of great activity on the Western Front, the great German offensive of the Spring having been repulsed with heavy casualties, and the Allies, reinforced with U.S. Army troops, and with increasing superiority in the air, sensing that the Germans were disintegrating in front of them. However the German troops had been ordered not to retire, and to fight to the last man.

On August 18th, after an intense series of trench raids, the 5th Division, of which the 1st Norfolks formed a part, moved south to an area East of Doullens, and North East of Amiens. Here a big advance was planned for August 21st. At zero hour (4.55.a.m.) on the day there was a thick mist, but the attack duly took place and was most successful, the objectives being carried in the face of determined German opposition. That night they were in a position near Achiet le Petit, but had lost two Captains and two Lieutenants wounded, as well as other ranks. The nights of 21st and 22nd were spent in consolidating the new positions, but during the 22nd the Germans responded with tremendous shell fire. Lieutenant Colonel Humphries, now commanding the battalion, and his adjutant, Captain Guy Tyler, were standing together and were mortally wounded by an exploding shell. Both died of their wounds soon after. Foncquevillers is a quiet village about 12 miles South East of Arras, and the British Military Cemetery is situated on the western outskirts of the village surrounded by fields. The graves of Guy Tyler and his colonel are side by side, together with other men of the 1st Norfolk Regiment. The cemetery is enclosed by a brick wall, and like all the cemeteries in France is beautifully kept.

Gravestone for Guy Cromwell Tyler, died August 1918.

Like all other deaths in action, Guy's death was a bitter blow to his family, and especially to his mother, who by August 1918 must have been increasingly hopeful that her beloved younger son might survive the dreadful war.

Guy Tyler, Adjutant the Norfolk Regt. shortly before he was killed in action.

Rosia and Wilfrid Fleming, probably in 1916.

These are two men who are linked to the Tyler family, and who I feel have a place in this book.

Wilfrid was one of a family of three children, having a sister Rosia, who married Oliver Tyler in 1927. Though this was ten years after Wilfrid was killed in action, he was Oliver's brother-in-law, and his wife Dorothy was always regarded as an Aunt by Oliver's children until she died. Oliver's eldest son was named Wilfrid in his memory.

Wilfrid Fleming was born in 1890, making him close in age to Oliver and Roland Tyler. His father had worked for many years in the Indian Civil Service, and served for some years in Burma. He was well off. Eventually they retired and came to live at Chagford in Devon, on the east side of Dartmoor. Here they had a comfortable and spacious house, with the summer house which would revolve and which fascinated me as a child. They could afford staff for house and garden, and had a large chauffeur driven car.

Wilfrid attended Harrow School, where he was a distinguished student, winning several prizes for reading. When he left Harrow at the age of 18, he entered the Royal Military Academy at Sandhurst, as he had decided on a career in the Army. He was duly gazetted Second Lieutenant and posted to the Devonshire Regiment in 1910.

Here he followed the usual routine of life as a junior infantry officer in peacetime England. Few could visualise that in just four years time a most terrible war would break out in Europe.

On the outbreak of war the Devonshire Regiment were among the first soldiers to be sent to France as part of "the first hundred thousand." It was truly being thrown in at the deep end. Interestingly, their first port of call en route was in Jersey. Was it on this occasion that Wilfrid first met Dorothy Fairlie, younger daughter of Lt. Colonel W.F. Fairlie? It was only a brief stop, however, for on 25th August the troops landed at Le Havre, and the move East to the front began, with Wilfrid's battalion ultimately joining the Lines of Communication Defence Troops.

Wilfrid was in the thick of the fighting from then on, and we know from the experience of Paul Archer May, also in the Devonshire Regiment, that the lifespan of a Lieutenant was very short. Moreover, the fact that Wilfrid was a regular officer with Sandhurst training would have made no difference, - German bullets and shells did not discriminate between one British junior officer and another in No Mans Land.

There is one clue to Wilfrid's survival at this time. In June 1915 Wilfrid was mentioned in Despatches and awarded the Military Cross for distinguished services in the Machine Gun Section. At the start of the Great War Machine Guns were regarded as new-fangled, unreliable and suspect. There was no true alternative to British rapid fire. Moreover Machine Guns were noisy, and likely to come to the attention of the enemy with resulting mortar and artillery fire which

Another superb Bairnsfather cartoon "Private Smith just keeping his hand in, to the dismay of his fellows."

upset the peace and tranquillity of a front line trench. The machine gunners were often "moved along" to someone else's trench

By 1915, however, the sight of vast swathes of advancing troops in Field Grey uniforms had convinced the allies of the value of the much improved machine guns as a vital weapon of defence, and they were carefully sited along the entire trench line, and their crews treated with great respect. Moreover, you did not send machine gun officers, especially those with an M.C. "over the top" to be mown down by a hail of bullets from their German counterparts.

German Machine Gun emplacement, Vimy Ridge.

Whatever, the true facts, Wilfrid survived, joining 14th Brigade, 5th Division on 30th September 1915, and then 95 Brigade, 5th Division on 12th January 1916. But by then he had set his sights on something a bit more exciting, and he became attached to the Royal Flying Corps, returning to Tidworth on Salisbury Plain to undergo flying training. The flying training log book belonging to Thomas May tells us exactly what that training would have consisted of, and how the young men went out on a wing and a prayer in flying machines held together with not much more than tape and string! Wilfrid returned as a qualified pilot to France in the spring of 1917. He had one other qualification as a result of his time in England. In the spring of 1917 he had married Dorothy Fairlie, though she would remain at her parent's house on the island of Jersey for the duration of the war and afterwards.

By the beginning of 1917, not only was the machine gun acknowledged as a vital weapon of modern warfare, but the aeroplane as well. By the end of 1917 the tank was to become the third member of the trio. Wilfrid joined 56 Squadron, RFC, and was stationed in North East France. The main duties were fighting with enemy aircraft, - at that point reckoned superior to our own, preventing them from carrying out observation sorties, and also doing reconnaissance work for our own artillery.

We have the pilots logs of patrols they did, and in particular Wilfrid's own section, flying from an aerodrome just to the west of Ypres. On August 10th 1917 six aircraft, all SE5s were sent out on patrol at different times of the

74

day, usually at least three aircraft at once to cover one another. Wilfrid took off at 12.50 p.m. for an OP patrol to the East in the Roulers-Menin-Contrae-Iseghem area. The official report of what happened was as follows:

"It was a bad day, with a lot of cloud and a forty mile wind blowing from the west, and it was his (Wilfrid Fleming's) first flight on an SE5 Aero. At about 1.p.m. his patrol was attacked by some eight German Albatross Scouts, and a sharp fight began, in the course of which our formation got scattered. On emerging from a cloud the patrol leader saw Fleming heavily engaged with three enemy planes far to the east. He was putting up a splendid fight, firing at close range at one of the enemy, while another of the Germans was close behind firing at him. The patrol leader went to his assistance, and together they so settled the Germans that they brought down one, and drove the others off. Then the leader and Fleming started to return home in the teeth of the wind, and in a bank of cloud the leader lost sight of Fleming. But from our aerodrome his machine was seen to land behind the German line, and it was thought he must have been forced down by lack of petrol. However, in January 1918 definite information came through that Fleming was killed in the action of August 10th and plane (sic) was buried in the cemetery of Ledeghan"

Two views of Sopwith Pup aircraft as flown by Wilfrid Fleming in 1917. This aircraft in Hendon Museum London & photographed in 2015.

His patrol leader wrote "It is a terrific loss to our squadron, and we are all very much upset about it. He was so popular with everyone. With a little more experience of air fighting he would have been absolutely invaluable, as he was such a good pilot."

There was a sad sequel to this account. The sentence "from our aerodrome his machine was seen to land behind the German line" seemed to suggest that the aircraft was under control, with the pilot still alive, though perhaps wounded, but that it landed rather than crashed. On October 14th 1917 Dorothy Fleming, Wilfrid's wife, wrote to a Major Blomfield from the address in Bristol where she was staying. Dorothy had noted that

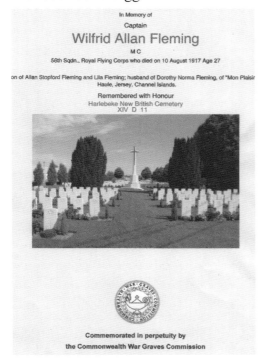

In Memory of
Captain
Wilfrid Allan Fleming
M C
56th Sqdn., Royal Flying Corps who died on 10 August 1917 Age 27

on of Allan Stopford Fleming and Lila Fleming; husband of Dorothy Norma Fleming, of "Mon Plaisir Haule, Jersey, Channel Islands.

Remembered with Honour
Harlebeke New British Cemetery
XIV D 11

Commemorated in perpetuity by
the Commonwealth War Graves Commission

Wilfrid Fleming is buried at Harlebeke New British Cemetery in North East France.

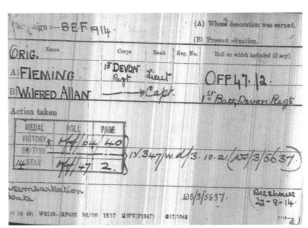

Capt. Wilfrid Allan Fleming, Devon Regt.

in the report on her husband's fate, he was not described as killed or wounded or lost in action. There was just a blank. Further, her cousin, Major Tod, also in the Royal Flying Corps had met a man who was at Wilfrid's aerodrome and who confirmed that Wilfrid's aircraft "was seen to land" – the wording of the report. Sadly for poor Dorothy his death was to be confirmed, though no details were ever given, and she became a widow some six months after her marriage, having only been with her husband for a few brief days. Sadly, she was far from alone in that tragic experience as a result of that horrific war.

In 1918, as the Germans were rolled back to their own borders, Wilfrid Flemings body was exhumed from its resting place in the German cemetery at Ledeghem and reburied at Harlebeke New British Cemetery. Several documents show how Dorothy had to make a choice over the inscription on his headstone. Wilfrid was 27 years old, the only son of his parents, and his sister Rosia was to die in tragic circumstances 17 years later.

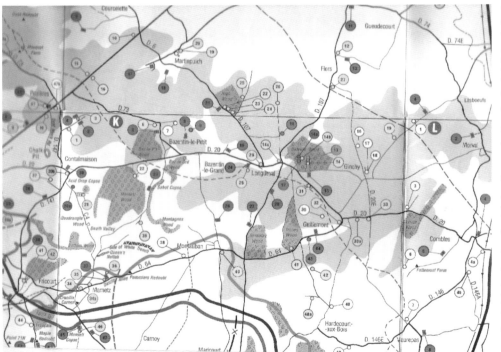

War map of the trenches and woods, Somme area 1916 – 1917.

Arthur Tyler Hitch was a first cousin to Oliver Tyler and his brothers, and I want to include him in this book for two reasons. First, he had a very distinguished career in the Infantry during the Great War, and second, because sadly he has no descendants. He was born in Bedfordshire in 1893, so was a little younger than the Tyler brothers, and he was 21 years old when the war started. He was put down for Officer Training, became a 2nd Lieutenant in the Bedfordshire Regiment, and went out to France in early 1915. He was soon promoted to full Lieutenant which was almost automatic in those grim days of infantry carnage.

Arthur served in the 6th Battalion of the Bedfordshire Regiment part of the 62nd Infantry Division. They were based in the area north of the river Somme, roughly between Albert and Arras. During the period June 1915 to March 1918 Arthur was closely involved in probably the most ferocious fighting on the whole Western Front, and must have been very lucky to survive. He was promoted to Captain, and then in 1917 to Major. He must have been fighting quite close to his Tyler cousins, but probably never met any of them.

Arthur Hitch, 2nd from right, with Tyler family members, about 1900.

The memorial to the Welsh Regiment at Mametz Wood, a very memorable place, photographed in 2015.

Fortunately his qualities as a soldier and leader were recognised, and it is unlikely that he had to lead men "over the top" after the Somme in 1916.

In the spring of 1918 the Germans mounted their great attack along the Western Front. with the twofold advantage of the collapse of Russia and consequent movement of troops from the east to the west, and also the mutiny of the French army. It was a desperate time, and the infantry bore the brunt of this offensive, with dreadful casualties.

On 1st April Arthur Hitch was promoted to the rank of temp. acting Lieutenant Colonel, and posted to be officer commanding the 8th Battalion of the Lincolnshire Regiment, part of the 63rd Infantry Brigade. They were located in the area around Havrincourt, Achiet-le-Grand and Achiet-le-Petit, and nearby Havrincourt Wood was to be the scene of prolonged fierce fighting as the Germans were driven back yard by yard. This wood was a German strong point, and had been heavily fortified. Extracts from the diary of the Brigade show in great detail how the advance was planned and executed.

Arthur Hitch as a child. C1897

Looking at the list of officers of the 8th Battalion, the Lincolnshire Regt, one is given a vivid insight into the progress of the war, and the characters and courage of the men who had survived into 1918. The chaplain was Captain T.B.Hardy, V.C. D.S.O. M.C. There were seven other captains, with a D.S.O. and two M.C.s There were ten Lieutenants, and 18 2nd Lieutenants, who had between them a further three M.C.s It is a very impressive list indeed.

On the 1st and 2nd of September 1918 the Battalion was resting, and Arthur Hitch organised two concerts for the men given by the Regimental Band. On Sept. 3rd their rest was over, and they marched by stages, reaching the N.W. corner of Havrincourt Wood on Sept. 5th, where they relieved 1st Battalion the Hertfordshire Regt. So far they had had no casualties. That changed significantly the next day, when they had one man killed and five wounded.

On Sept. 7th " A Coy. Pressed forward to Shropshire Reserve, C. Coy. Formed line of parts from Junction of Henly Lane and Cheetham Swith to junction Hubert Av. And Shropshire Reserve. Btn. H.Q. moved up to W. End of wood

A page from the war diary of the Lincolnshire Regiment, whose Colonel was Arthur Hitch at this time.

at K.36.D. 40. 30. Casualties 7 Other Ranks wounded. Heavy shelling with sneezing (?) gas etc." On September 8th C. Coy pushed forward to Cheetham Switch, and suffered 2 more killed and 4 wounded.

On 9th Sept. they relieved the 1st Essex Regiment, and C Coy ended up at Yorkshire Heap. They had 1 man killed, 5 wounded and 9 gassed. The names given to the trenches and areas are fascinating, and reflect where the troops came from who named them. On Sept 10th they captured an enemy Machine Gun, took two prisoners and killed eight of the enemy. But they had 2nd Lieut G. Jones killed plus 5 other ranks, nine men wounded and 3 gassed. Capturing the wood was a very costly undertaking.

Colonel Arthur Hitch DSO war record document for medals dated 1921.

The only known photograph of Arthur Hitch in uniform, probably about 1915.

After 3 rest and training days, Sept. 12th to 14th, the Battalion were subjected to an enemy counter attack which was beaten back, but resulted in 6 men wounded. There were a further 9 casualties the next day. On the 22nd, after days of heavy fighting, the battalion received 63 men as reinforcements, and Captain Gary was awarded the M.C.

On 30th September the Division was moved to Ruyaulcourt, as part of the general advance taking place, and they were congratulated by their general on a job very well done. Col. Arthur Hitch was awarded the D.S.O and the citation read "For conspicuous gallantry and good leadership in the operations about Havrincourt Wood in the period 9th and 10th Sept 1918. He personally supervised the pushing forward of the line north of the wood over ground which was under very heavy shell fire. Throughout the operations he handled his battalion with great skill, courage and judgement. His good leadership, and personal disregard of danger during a difficult period of wood fighting contributed largely to the rapid retreat of the enemy and the complete success of the days operations."

There are further documents which detail the Battalion's activities during the month of Sept. 1918, and these will have continued until the signing of the Armistice on 11th November. The opposition of German troops became ever more desperate as they were pushed back towards the border of Belgium, France and Germany, and Arthur Hitch, as a senior officer would have found his work ever more demanding, despite the huge boost to morale consequent upon the well-founded belief that the Allies were at last winning the war.

Arthur Hitch in the 1960s, keeping an eye on the croquet.

The available papers do not give the date that Arthur Hitch was eventually demobbed, but he was making application for his war medals and emblems in early 1921. There was one other very significant result of Arthur's distinguished war service.

Catherine Williams was born in 1900, and was a very petite young lady, full of spirit. By 1917, at the age of 17, she joined a nursing service, and was posted to France where she drove military ambulances. Those of us who knew her, and who also know what a First World War Ambulance was like, will find this almost unbelievable! How she had the strength to wrestle such a heavy vehicle along the appalling roads behind the trenches in Flanders and France is amazing, but she was obviously both brave and inspirational.

During those last months of the war "Billie," as she was always known, met Colonel Arthur Hitch, and it seems to have been love at first sight, perhaps as a result of the single minded patriotism and courage of both of them combined with a strong physical attraction. They soon married, and enjoyed a long and very happy marriage, but sadly were not able to have any children.

It seems most appropriate that Colonel Arthur Hitch's war record should be included in this account of the war, because he was such a distinguished officer and leader of men.

Arthur and Billie Hitch at Elm Park probably in the early 1960s.

CHAPTER EIGHT.
PAUL ARCHER MAY. THOMAS RATCLIFFE AGNEW MAY 1916 – 1918

War map of area fought over by the Devon Regiment 1915-1917

Paul May was sixteen when the war started, and he was being educated at Marlborough College, thanks to the generosity and support of his father's relatives. His letters from school show him to have been happy with his situation, though not an academic high flyer. Marlborough College, like all the great English Public Schools, had a very strong link with the services, with an officer training corps, led by masters who had been in the armed forces. Regularly old boys from the school would appear in their various uniforms, to keep younger boys spellbound with their perhaps slightly exaggerated tales of military life. Of course since August 1914 these accounts had revolved around the Great War, and a keen observer would have noted how in the years immediately following August 1914 the reports had changed, the early optimism being replaced by a sad and often tragic realism. Meanwhile the list of Old Boys who had been either killed or wounded in battle grew ever longer.

In the current atmosphere at Marlborough, there was only one immediate destiny for Paul May, given his home upbringing in the village where his father, the Rector, was already visiting new widows whose husbands or other family members had been recently killed. A friend, Canon Wynne Wilson, nominated Paul for officer training at Sandhurst, which was a much sought after opportunity to enter the army as an officer, and Paul transferred to Sandhurst in November 1915 to begin his training. On August 16th 1916, as the first battle of the Somme raged in France, Paul was commissioned 2nd Lieutenant, and Gazetted to the 3rd (Reserve) Battalion of the Devonshire Regiment. The period from August 1916 to February 1917 was spent in further training at the 3rd Devons main depot at North Raglan Barracks, Devonport, Plymouth.

Sandhurst, and the training that followed, seem to have been a happy time for Paul, despite the continuing news from the front. The war was still some distance away, and a number of people still expected it to be over following a great and decisive battle. Paul seems to have got on very well with his brother soldiers, and his childhood training would have helped a lot. There was a very strong camaraderie among the men as they trained, knowing that the life of each might depend on the actions of his fellow soldiers.

Paul May during training.1916.

Incidentally, this was the same Regiment in which Wilfrid Fleming served, though he was shortly to transfer to the Royal Flying Corps.

Meanwhile Paul was able to continue normal family activities, and Devonport was not so far from Bodmin with a good train service to Bodmin Road station on the dependable Great Western Railway. From the station it was a reasonable walk home for a fit soldier. As shown there are a number of photographs of Paul in his officers uniform at home with his father. From home he wrote to his sister Grace a birthday letter on November 12th 1915: "This is just a line to wish you many happy returns of your birthday. Things seem to go on just the same as usual. Doney (The coachman/gardener) went to fetch Pat as there was torrents of rain here. So he wanted me to feed the fowls which I promised faithfully to do. Of course I forgot about the fowls and the ferrets." I bet he got an earful from Doney on his return, officer or whatever!

His father wrote to him regularly at the barracks. Paul had been on a bomb throwing course. His father wanted to know if this just covered the principles of the warfare, or did they actually practice throwing the bombs? Did they learn all about the mechanism of the infernal machines? Again "What do you think of your last month's mess bill? To us it seems pretty high!" It was very difficult not to spend money in the mess when all those around you were doing so, and you were expected to buy your round. But then most soldiers' fathers earned a lot more than the rector of a very small Cornish parish.

2nd *Lt. Paul May,*
Devonshire Regt.

   The training continued, and Paul learned about the very proud history of the Devonshire Regiment, from its founding under King James II in 1685 to the present day. It's battle honours read like a summary of British history, including the campaigns of the Duke of Marlborough, The Napoleonic War, especially in the Peninsula, Afghanistan and India, and the Boer War, especially at Ladysmith. In the present war the Regiment had distinguished itself at Ypres, Loos and on the Somme.

Paul May's life was changed once and for all when he landed in France on 3rd February, 1917. He was following in the footsteps of millions of his countrymen who had made the crossing of the channel, and who never returned. On February 19th he joined the famous 1st Battalion of the Devonshire Regiment, who were closely engaged with the enemy in the region around Lens, in North West France.

The reality of this grim world can be easily understood from the War Diary of the 1st Battalion. Quite apart from the weather, cold and wet much of the time, and the lack of sleep, there was constant tension with attacks being mounted, counter attacks being repulsed, outpost picket duty, sentry duty, and raiding parties, all to the accompaniment of enemy shelling and gas attacks. Every day there were casualties, but when an attack was mounted to try and win a few yards of enemy held territory they were enormous.

On one day, April 23rd 1917, the Battalion lost 3 officers killed in action, with 8 others wounded seriously, and two missing. Forty other ranks were killed that day, with a further 29 missing, and 157 wounded. Five were wounded but continued on duty.

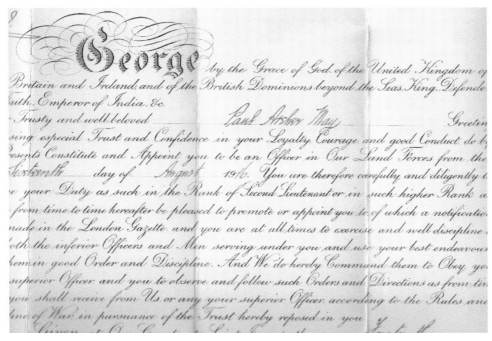

Paul May Commission Warrant from King George V. 1917.

The diary records as follows: "Trenches. 14th April. At 5.a.m the Battalion moved forward to the line S.6.Central – s,5,b,9,8. where it was held up by rifle and M.G. fire from the LA COULOTTE – Electric Generating Station Line. Nos 1 and 2 Coys were on the front line, Nos 3 and 4 Coys in support, Headquarters in CLICK TRENCH. During the night Nos 3 and 4 Coys were withdrawn to CLICK TRENCH and Nos 1 and 2 Coys took up outpost positions slightly to the W. of extreme point of advance. Connection was established with the 1st Battn Cheshire Regt., (15th Infantry Brigade) on our right, and 1st Battn. D.C.L.I. on our left. 2nd Lieut S.M.Neilson and 5 other ranks killed in action. Capt. J.L. Veitch and 32 other ranks wounded. 11 other ranks joined as reinforcements from base."

2ⁿᵈ. Lt. Paul May with his father and 2 fellow officers.

There is one rather curious incident recorded on a small sheet of paper, perhaps torn out of a notebook. It reads : "Paul was crossing the green on Vimy and they (many) were firing all round him for he had his hands in his pockets, & he turned round and faced them and in a loud voice you could hear a long distance now said "Kill me if you want to" and every gun ceased firing & he slowly walked back with his hands in his pockets, looking a huge figure." This must be an eyewitness account, and refer to Paul May, for it is included with his surviving papers. It is unclear why Paul did this, for I am sure it would not have been pure bravado. It does place Paul near Vimy Ridge, a famous location in the war, and close to the last fighting he was engaged in.

Paul May's last letter home was written in April 12ᵗʰ, on a page torn out of a field dispatch book. It reads " Dearest dad and Mother, I have received your letter posted on 5ᵗʰ April. We have had some bad weather again, a lot of snow and rain. We are now under canvass and quite happy. I am quite well, and have had a cake from Aunt Ada, which arrived the same day as your parcel. Hope Tom is alright again. Yrs Paul. P.T.O. P.S. In the next parcel you might send me some pasties, proper ones, not too salt, farmhouse style, as the rest of the officers want to know what

Paul May's last letter home, with a request for Cornish pasties.

they are like. I am sure Hilda knows how to make them." Alas, the pasties were never sent, so his brother officers remained in ignorance.

The war diary continues: "Trenches. 15th April. Situation remained unchanged. Patrols kept contact with the enemy. Positions were intermittently shelled by the enemy during the day. The 1st Battalion Cheshire Regt. On our right were relieved by the 1st Battalion the Norfolk Regt. (15th Infantry Brigade.) 2nd Lieut. P.A.May and 2 other ranks killed in action. 15 other ranks wounded."

Page from War Diary recording Paul May killed. April 1917.

It is suggested by another source that Paul was killed during the night of April 14/15 but whether it was an enemy shell, or during a raid we shall never know. He was just 19 years old, and his death bears out the fact that it was the junior officers leading their infantryman into battle who were the most likely to be killed. The note I have states that Paul May was buried near the Bois de la Hirondelles, south west of Lens. His grave is not marked or known, and his name is inscribed on the huge war memorial in Arras, dedicated to those who have no known grave. In situations of such devastating sadness those involved try to offer what comfort they can. The family received several letters from Pauls regimental comrades, and someone, probably his mother, wrote an appreciation for the Marlborough College magazine.

In Memory of
Second Lieutenant
Paul Archer May

1st Bn., Devonshire Regiment who died on 15 April 1917 Age 19

Son of the Rev. Frederick Granville May and Dora Kate May, of Springfield Tuckenhay, Totnes, Devo

Remembered with Honour
Arras Memorial

moved after the war

The Arras General War Memorial.

"The brother officers of the Battalion wrote of their comrade with the greatest affection. And regret at his early loss, and said that the loyalty of his men and what we, his brother officers know of him are proof that he was a soldier and gentleman to the end. He was much loved and respected as a good and conscientious leader and a very brave and gallant officer. We have indeed suffered a great loss."

The Colonel of the 3rd Reserve Battalion, the Devonshire Regiment wrote to Mrs May on April 27th 1917: "Dear Mrs May, I am very grieved to hear you have lost your eldest son in action. He served in the Battalion under my command, until he joined the Expeditionary Force, and was a great favourite with us all. He always performed his duties most conscientiously, and was a first rate officer. Nothing ever seemed to put him out, - he was so good tempered and had such a nice disposition. With my deepest sympathy with you and your family."

A letter from a sergeant in Pauls company says: "I am speaking on behalf of the men of my platoon, and I myself, when I send you the heartfelt sympathy of us all. He had no regard for his personal safety, - his motto was 'look after the men first' and he was beloved by us all."

Paul Archer May served in France for just over two months, during which time he obviously made a deep impression on those he served with, both officers and men. This story emphasises the short life expectations for an Infantry Second Lieutenant, and the shocking waste in human lives resulting from this devastating war.

TOM R.A.MAY. ROYAL FLYING CORPS. 1917 – 1918.

Tom May in flying kit while in training.

Tom May, at Sherborne School, must have felt the loss of his brother Paul very keenly. He was nearly 18 years old, and nearing the end of his school days. He left school in the July, and immediately joined the Royal Naval Air Service, soon to become the Royal Flying Corps. It must have been very hard for his parents, now both about 62 years old, to have their second and now only son going into the services so soon. Yet everyone now expected it, and I am sure Tom felt it was the right course of action, and his way of avenging his brothers early sacrifice and death.

And it is obvious that Tom was captivated by the thought of becoming a pilot. In the three years from 1914 to 1917 flying had been revolutionised. Planes had become much more sophisticated, and faster. Weaponry had improved greatly. Above all, the role of aircraft in warfare was not only acknowledged, but the opportunities for aircraft to affect the outcome of conflict on the ground was growing by the day.

Having finished his basic training, Tom May was posted to Manston Royal Naval Flying School, in east Kent, in October 1917, and he experienced his first flight on October 13th, flying dual control in a MF 5728 aircraft. After four flights in the week, practising "straights" and "turns" he had logged 1 hour 4 minutes flying time. This was certified by a senior officer, and it was this total of flying hours which was the key assessment throughout his period of training.

After a week's break, probably for other training, he and his instructor practised landings, surely one of the most important challenges for any pilot! We shall see how important these landing always were during the period of training.

Paul had been able to slip home from Devonport, on a regular basis, but Tom May, based in the far east of Kent, had no such opportunity. However, he continued to be a good letter writer, especially to his sister Grace, when she was at school at Salisbury, and also to his parents and several aunts. Many of his letters survive and make fascinating reading.

Meanwhile, Tom continued with his training, and it is interesting and a little worrying to see from his log book how quickly he was introduced to simple aerobatics and take offs, and on 6th November he did his first solo flight of 7 minutes, at 200 feet in the MF5728. That

Pages from Tom May's pilot training log book 1917.

same afternoon, a few minutes later, he did a second solo flight, reaching 1600 feet, and flying solo for 23 minutes. By the end of the week his total flying hours were 5 hrs 44 minutes dual, and 30 minutes solo. One gets the impression that he was very competent and most enthusiastic. He wrote to his parents "I had another 1 hour dual

Tom May in R.N. Air Service uniform.

today, and then went up solo for seven minutes. I was so successful that when I came down he sent me up again and I was up for 23 minutes and climbed to 1600 feet. It was grand!"

Later in the same letter Tom records "There was a horrid crash here last Sunday. One of the Handley Pages fell and caught on fire, and 3 people were burnt to death, and 2 injured. It was due to carelessness as they went up with the aileron controls locked so that the pilot was quite helpless. I.P.F.O was burnt. Of course the pilot ought to have tested the controls before starting." No wonder Tom's parents had completely white hair by this time!

Reading Tom's logbook it soon becomes apparent that the pilots faced one most important problem, and that was unreliable engines. On November 12th he was practising circuits, but "only doing 1650 revs with throttle fully open."

Later on the 12th he went as passenger to fetch another machine. "Engine stopped twice, and was missing all the time on 2 cylinders." One must remember that at this time no pilots had parachutes, so if your engine stopped you had to hope you could glide down and find somewhere for a reasonably soft landing.

On November 30th Tom achieved his record height so far, but "engine still doing only 1650. Vibrations broke the rev counter. Did two good landings." On December 4th he had his Passing Out Test – "Flew a straight, 2 turns and a landing. Landed alright, but a bit of a pancake. Comment, 'Alright, but rather too hard on the rudder.' Two days later he flew an Avro for the first time. By the end of the week of December 14th, his total solo was 8 hours 12 minutes. But in that week he did no flying. There is then a very curious gap in his flying, with apparently no flying at all until April 12th 1918. However, two letters dated 29.1.18 and 30.1.17 (sic) from "Zymotics, R.N.Hospital, Chatham" suggest that Tom was in the hospital and suffering from some illness, not the result of a plane crash! There were four chaps in his small room, and he says "only one chap is bad, he still has the rash badly, and the other three, including me, are more or less convalescent and we have chats and games of draughts etc." His main need was for oranges or tangerines, and for needles for his gramophone, - His Masters Voice were expensive so Columbia or Zonophone would do! When Tom flew again on 12th April 1918 he records "got on better than I expected having not flown for 5 months. Whatever the illness was, it put him out of action for a surprisingly long period.

Tom did these first flights with an instructor in the machine. He records "Engine vibrating badly, so came down for a new machine. Found taxiing difficult, being too slow on the rudder. Got very stale towards the end, and did two bad landings. Felt quite confident in the air." He then had a break of 10 days before he flew again, and on April 26th "the petrol tank stopper came out, so went in for new machine." Having petrol slopping out all over the aircraft must have been highly undesirable.

…Flying the Avro several times the inlet valve blew out, and it could be a very bumpy ride. After one landing in a ploughed field, which he considered good, he failed to take off properly, the "engine choked, tried to sideslip into a field, let the nose down and crashed." One feels relieved that his family did not read the daily reports in the log book, as they would have aged his poor parents

"Bad luck on Lincoln!" Tom May's log book 1918.

drastically!

By the time Tom had done 34 hours of solo flying it was May 22nd, and he was posted up to the Royal Air Force Flying School at Cranwell in Lincolnshire and had changed to a Sopworth Pup aircraft. It did not go all that smoothly, and he burst several tyres. Eventually "When I reached 200 feet the engine cut out (high tension lead off) landed in a hayfield, burst two tyres. Very good landing considering circumstances." It seems amazing that he seems to have come through unscathed so far.

Tom was now let loose to fly further afield, sometimes being able to see where he was going, and sometimes not. Twice he made emergency landings in fields. On 29th May he did a solo flight in the Sopworth Pup and took a route to Grantham, Newark, Lincoln, and back to Cranwell. He records "Did two rolls and three loops over Lincoln and was then sick. Steered by compass." Someone, presumably his senior officer, has ringed this entry in pencil, and written at the side "Bad luck on Lincoln."!

Aircraft typical of those flown by Tom May during his training.

On May 18th Tom wrote a very interesting letter to his sister Grace, then at school. "I flew an Avro with a Le Rhone engine in it last night, and they are vastly superior to the ordinary Gnomes – fly much quicker and are much more reliable. I am probably going on Scout machines, but nothing is settled yet. We have cabins here at Cranwell with 2 in each, which is a great improvement on the Manston dormitories. I went to church parade this morning. They had a ripping band, and quite a nice service. Prince Albert was on parade, and I saw Prince Henry afterwards. They both look to me most slim and watery youths." Tom was not one to talk, judging by his photographs, but one wonders what the two princes were doing at Cranwell. Prince Albert (later George VI) went into the Navy, I think. Meanwhile the flying training continued. He did a "height test. Spun down 4000 feet and made myself sick. Good landing." Well, it's how you eventually come down that matters, and Lincoln was spared this time. I wonder if those strolling round the aerodrome always carried erect umbrellas? Tom moved on to flying the famous Sopworth Camel, and on 1st June took off for his longest solo flight to date. It is worth quoting from his logbook in full as this gives a very fair idea of what an adventure flying was at this time. He took off at about 5.p.m.

The record in Tom May's logbook of his hair raising cross country flight, which just ended alright! 1918.

" Visibility very poor, and thick haze over everything, particularly when steering E-W. Departed on cross country to Boston, struck the coast just north of it and steered south 'til I struck the town. From there steered W.W.W. for a considerable time but did not see any landmark, so turned a steered East to test compass. Arriving at the coast north of Boston was satisfied compass was reasonably correct. Started again, steering a bit more to the north, and eventually struck Lincoln. Recognised the town, and steered S.S.W. and after flying some time petrol in pressure tank gave out and so did a good pancake in a cornfield to find myself 40 miles south of Boston. Obtained help, and wheeled machine out of cornfield, switched to gravity tank and started again, steering NW. After flying 40 minutes arrived at Sleaford, expecting petrol to give out any minute and not wishing to land without the engine, with the gravity tank empty came down in a hayfield. Had to make a very fast landing owing to machine being very nose heavy, but brought it off very well. Wired for petrol which duly arrived, and took off in

95

the dusk at 10.p.m. Swerved rather and just managed to hoik machine over a hedge. Arrived at aerodrome at 10.08 and made a very good landing in the semi-darkness."

On the 3rd of June he did a trip of 90 minutes from Cranwell to Lincoln, Newark, Grantham, Spalding, Boston, Sleaford and back to base, without any forced landings or running out of petrol, and wrote "Followed this course well with the help of map. Did a good landing." He was flying at 3,000 feet in a Sopworth Camel again. His superior officer signed off Tom's week with the comment "you should try to write a book of flying experiences!!!!" By now Tom had flown 56 hours solo.

There could still be problems. On June 6th he wrote "Intended going on cross country to Nottingham, but engine conked. Made a good landing two miles south of aerodrome, near Alchester Road." Tom does not say how his aircraft, or bits of it, were recovered, but I suppose at least they were pretty light in weight! Tom now started practising for combat, and again there could be problems. He notes "one gun had defective feed block, and the other jammed three times." Aerial gunnery was still very much in it's infancy.

By June 24th he was learning formation flying and how to attack other aircraft in the air, splitting up formations of "enemy" aircraft, or taking on single machines. On the 26th he "did some low flying down in front of hangers with climbing turns. Attacked D.H.9 with fair success. Very heavy landing."

Between July 15th and August 2nd Tom May was posted to the Gunnery School at Freiston, where he flew the Sopworth Camel and learned Ground Gunnery, Aerial Gunnery and Aerial Fighting. He used Vickers and Lewis Machine Guns, and in the three categories scored 91%, 70%, and 83%, with an overall average of 81%. He was given the qualification V.G. His total flying time to date was about 90 hours. Curiously, Tom's logbook records 10 flights between July 20th and August

2Lt. Tom May, Royal Flying Corps, in flying kit, August 1918, shortly before he was killed.

1st. These involved aerial combat tactics, firing guns and formation flying. By August 1st, when the logbook finishes, Tom had logged 10 hours dual and 79 ½ hours solo flying.

Tom does not seem to have been granted any home leave before being posted to France, - perhaps the need for aircraft in the front line was desperate at this time. On August 7th he posted a postcard to his parents from Dover, showing a picture of the very grand Hotel Burlington. He wrote "Just had lunch here, leaving by destroyer for Dunkirk at 4,30. this afternoon. Am not appointed to a squadron yet, will find out address and add in pencil. Aunt Kate said she would write all the news. Letter follows at first opportunity."

Tom was as good as his word, and wrote from 5 Group Pilots Pool, R.A.F., B.E.F. France,

Tom May report from Gunnery School. 1918.

presumably on August 8th. He wrote a long letter " Dear Mother and Dad, I have at last got to some more or less permanent resting place probably for a fortnight before going to a squadron." Tom goes on to detail shopping in Piccadilly, and trying to meet up with his Uncle Charles. Having succeeded he then had to go and get his orders, and then went with Uncle Charles to Weybridge for the night. He met several members of the family, and after an early night his cousin Rebecca accompanied him to Town and saw him off at Victoria. He spent the afternoon with a friend in the lounge of the Burlington Hotel. Later they embarked for France.

" The sea was as smooth as glass, and you would not know you were on it unless you got in the wash of one of the destroyers. The passage only took 2 hours, and I did not feel in the least ill. We had an excellent meal on

*Tom May's last postcard home
to his parents, August 7ᵗʰ.1918.*

board, still I should have like to go by destroyer." (Was he on a ferry of some sort?) When Tom got ashore he says the roads were bad and he was rather disappointed in France, - no hedges and very dirty. "I fancy every now and then I can hear guns this morning, I wonder if it really is, we must be nearly 60 miles from the firing line, double the distance we expected."

Tom planned to go to Calais to change money when opportunity permitted. No flying in prospect, as the weather bad. "I have all I want so far except my fountain pen. The haversack and waterproof sheet not required. You will not want another letter for a week, unless there are special developments while I am here as there are not likely to be any special interests or excitements here. I will try to do right. Your loving son, Tom. R.A.May."

I do not know whether his parents received this letter before or after the terrible telegram telling them Tom had died on August 9ᵗʰ.

I have speculated that on August 9ᵗʰ Tom May was issued with an aircraft from the Pool, and that it was a sort of initiation rite that he should take it up and give a demonstration of his flying skills to his fellow pilots. There is evidence from another source that this was the custom. It is backed up by the letter to someone known to Tom's parents written by a fellow pilot, and dated August 25ᵗʰ 1918.

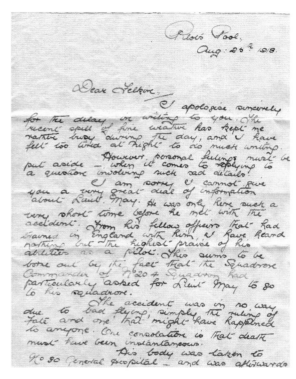

The letter explaining how Tom May's accident occurred on August 9th 1918.

"Dear Felkire,

I apologise sincerely for the delay in writing to you. The recent spell of fine weather has kept me rather busy during the day, and I have been too tired at night to do much writing. However, personal feelings must be put aside, when it comes to replying to a question which involves such sad details. I am sorry I cannot give you a very great deal of information about Lieut. May. He was only here for such a very short time before he met with the accident. From his fellow officers who had trained in England with him, I have heard nothing but the highest praise for his abilities as a pilot. This seems to be borne out by the fact that the Squadron Commander of No. 204 Squadron had particularly asked for Lieut. May to go to his squadron.

The accident was in no way due to bad flying, simply the ruling of fate and one that might have happened to anyone. One consolation is that death must have been instantaneous. His body was taken to No. 30 General Hospital, and was afterwards buried in that little cemetery on the outskirts of Calais, on the road to Sangatte.

Again apologising for the delay, I remain yours V. Sincerely, L.C.H.Slatter."

Letters of condolence came to his shattered parents from fellow pilots, family and friends, and even from the headmaster of Sherborne School, Cecil Nowell Smith. The headmaster had hoped that Tom would train to be a doctor, and had offered to help with the school fees, anonymously, because he considered Tom such a promising pupil. But for Fred and Kate May there was no consolation for the loss of their two sons in a matter of 18 months, nor for the fact that Tom had only survived in France for two days.

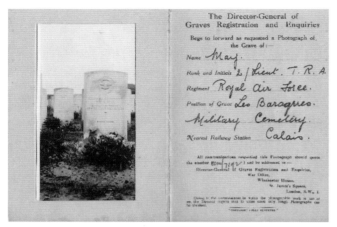

It is very easy to overlook the small cemetery at Sangatte. Fortunately one of our party spotted the small direction notice on a wall in what is a built up area and part of the suburbs of Calais these days. The cemetery, like all of them, is beautifully maintained. They were mowing the lawns while we were there. Tom's headstone records:

"In memory of Second Lieut. Thomas Radcliffe Agnew May, No.4. Aircraft Supply Depot, Royal Air Force, who died on 09 August 1918 aged 19 years. Son of Rev. F.G. and D.K.May of Cardynham Rectory, Bodmin, Cornwall. Remembered with Honour. Les Baraques Military Cemetery, Sangatte."

Communion Rail in Cardynham Church given in memory of 2Lt. Tom May, R.F.C.

Two views of Tom May's headstone in Sangatte Cemetery, Calais, one taken in 1918 and one in 2015.

Walter and Lil Tyler at Wormley, in about 1930.

Walter and Elizabeth Tyler had borne the stress of having all their three sons fighting in the fiercest part of the action for the entire war. Guy, Lil's beloved youngest son had been badly wounded, but against all his mother's hopes and probably arguments he had returned to the hellish fighting and been killed in the most gruesome manner a few months before the war ended. Roland had already returned to India, and when he was demobbed would presumably pick up the threads of his life there as it was before 1914.

Oliver returned to England in April 1919, having spent the best part of six months helping with the unpleasant and often dangerous task of clearing up the battlefields. He found the "land fit for heroes" sadly lacking. Almost every household had been directly or indirectly affected by the four years of war. Sergeant John Lawley of the Royal Warwickshire Regiment was killed fighting in Flanders on 23rd May 1918 at the age of 37 years. Needless to say he was the breadwinner for his family, and a grateful nation granted his widow a pitifully small pension to bring up her five young children, one of whom was my wife's mother.

Grave of Sergeant John Lawley photographed in 2015.

Over the whole country lay a pall of bereavement and exhaustion. The national economy was in ruins, and politicians seemed unable to decide on any course for the future. Meanwhile the surrender terms imposed on Germany were unrealistic and humiliating. Shipyard workers in Hamburg watched with tears streaming down their faces as their newly completed liner "Imperator" was seized as a war reparation and was to become the flagship of the British Cunard Line, renamed the Berengaria after an early English Queen. This situation boded very ill for the future.

R.M.S.Berengaria, formerly "Imperator" the new flagship of the Cunard Line in 1919.

In Wormley Oliver Tyler found a very depressing situation. Instead of being thankful that two of her sons had survived the dreadful conflict, Lil could not understand how the older boys could have allowed their baby brother to die and be buried in a foreign field. His room in the house had been turned into a shrine where nothing must ever be touched.

His name could only be mentioned in a hushed whisper. Oliver could not cope with it, and he escaped down to the Salcombe Estuary as soon as he could. He could have stayed at Ferryside with David Roberts, or in the house anyway. Sailing in the yawl "May" in such beautiful surroundings he could forget both his present problems and the horrors of war. In fact, like the vast majority of his forces comrades, he coped by wiping from his memory all the events of those appalling four years. He never talked about it, and it was as if it had never happened.

But what to do with himself? Now thirty one years old, with excellent engineering qualifications and an experience second to none, he longed to build a career and settle down, marry and raise a family. While at

back to his days as a dispatch rider. He and Sylvia had two children, Guy and Shirley, born in the late 1920s and early 30s. Tragically, Guy was to die of polio just after the second world war, and Shirley never married.

The marriage of Oliver Tyler and Rosia Fleming at Chagford in 1927. Grace May is second from the right.

Oliver was determined that when he married, his new bride should come out to Kenya to find a worthy house waiting for her, and he set to work, largely with his own hands, to bring this about. Meanwhile an increasingly frustrated Rosia wrote to him to remind him that she was not getting any younger, and how much longer was the house going to take?

Oliver and Rosia were married at Chagford on June 22nd 1927, and one of their bridesmaids was Grace May, a keen Girl Guide like Rosia. They then had an extended honeymoon motoring round the Lake District and Scotland. Both Oliver and Rosia drove the Morris Cowley with enthusiasm. In the late summer the couple returned to Kenya, and Rosia was introduced to her new home. M'Sitoni was sited on an East facing slope on the South East side of Molo township, and there was plenty of scope for creating a garden. Oliver, with his love of horses and ponies, had provided a range of four stables behind the house on the rising ground. Both he and Rosia did a lot of exploring on horseback.

Oliver and Rosia on honeymoon in the Lake District driving a Morris Cowley in 1927.

Oliver, Rosia and children boating on Lake Naivasha, in Kenya, c 1932.

Oliver and transport for two very young children, Molo, Kenya, 1934.

Wilfrid must have almost been a honeymoon baby, being born at the end of April 1928. How far away the war must have seemed to both Oliver and Rosia by this time. They lived in a new world, much of which Oliver and his partners had created. Both of them got on very well with the native Kenyans, and in due course Oliver was to design and build three churches. Jennifer was to be born in late 1929, and Diana in 1931. Kenya was growing and developing as an exciting and increasingly prosperous country, and it was people like Oliver and his partners who were laying down an infrastructure for the future.

As the family grew in size, so the house needed to do the same. The design was a simple one, and it was comparatively easy, given Oliver's engineering expertise, to build on a second house attached to the first giving the extra necessary sleeping accommodation. Oliver was proving a more and more skilled carpenter, and not only did house building, but furniture and even children's toys as well, some of which have survived to this day in the households of his descendants.

Molo Church built by Oliver in 1932, exterior and interior views.

Right. Oliver and Rosia on ponies.

Meanwhile back in Hertfordshire, Walter and 'Lil must have led a rather sad life. The shadow of the Great War still hung over their home. As stated, Oliver did come back to England on a

Walter & Lil, Roly & Sylvia.

Sylvia Tyler, Guy & Shirley

regular basis, but there were other people and places he also wanted to visit. By the time their first grandchild was born, Walter was 69 years old, and his wife a little younger, and they would be destined because of geography to see very little of their grandchildren, for Roland and Sylvia were settled down in South Devon by the time their children were born. Roland kept his business interests in London, which necessitated regular visits, but he and Sylvia loved the Salcombe estuary, and were always out and about in boats. Sylvia in particular loved fishing, and was always setting "spillers" – night lines, for which she had to dig quantities of lug worms as bait. Her rather strange detached kitchen at "Ferryside" always had a decidedly fishy smell, whatever she was cooking. Shirley, her daughter, very much took after her mother as she grew up. Roland used to smoke a pretty powerful pipe to mask other odours that were floating past!

Shirley & Guy Tyler

It was truly an idyllic place to live, right beside the waters of the estuary. Guy was born in 1926, and Shirley four years later in 1930. As the 1930s passed, Roland, Guy and Shirley became more involved in sailing and boating activities in the harbour, especially in school holidays. Sylvia ran the estate, supervising the gardens, keeping a flock of hens and looking after several ponies and horses in the fields. She never learned to drive, except to drive their motor boat, "Molly", and always seemed a very kind, tolerant and contented person.

Page from Rose Cottage visitors book.

Rose Cottage, Instow. 1932.

Instow beach, 1932, with Oliver, Rosia, Wilfrid and other friends.

As the business in Kenya thrived, Oliver could afford to bring his whole family back to England, and in 1932 he rented a house called Rose Cottage, at Instow in North Devon, for about six weeks in the summer. Instow is a beautiful spot, close to the junction of the Taw and Torridge rivers, before they flow out into the sea, and between Bideford and Barnstable. Several people took the opportunity to come and stay with the family, including Walter and 'Lil, Mrs Fleming, Rosia's mother, and Katherine Parker and Grace May, Rosia's Girl Guide friends from Devon.   As it turned out, this holiday was a very fortunate event, for Oliver did not feel well and went to consult a doctor. He was at once referred to a specialist, who diagnosed testicular cancer, and an urgent operation was performed at Moreton Hampstead hospital, not far away. It was a complete success, but Oliver must have spent a good deal of the holiday convalescing. It was a good thing that the various visitors were able to help Rosia looking after the children, and doing tasks around the house,

Oliver & Children. Molo 1934

as good Girl Guides always would. Oliver made a complete recovery and went on to have six more children.

The family returned to Kenya in September, and all Oliver's enterprises continued to thrive, and to crown his happiness Rosia again became pregnant at the end of 1933. But disaster and tragedy came suddenly out of a clear blue sky. The twins, Norman and Nicholas, were born on July 12th 1934. The following day their mother died, probably as a result of inadequate medical care and facilities. When, as a result of the aftermath of the war, many younger people went to fairly remote places to try and build new lives, they often ended up living in countries where medical facilities were sparse or even non-existent. In the early 1930s penicillin was unknown, and fighting infection was a matter of nursing skills and hospital facilities. Moreover, in tropical countries infections would grow more quickly. Rosia was buried in the main churchyard in the city of Nakuru, and Oliver's life, was shattered, together with that of his five children.

Rosia Tyler's gravestone, Nakuru, 2008, with Rachel, her granddaughter touching up the lettering.

CHAPTER TEN. THE MAY FAMILY. 1918 – 1936.

Rev. F.G.May, Kate May and Grace in early 1920s, with Theo the dog.

Nowhere was the aftermath of the War felt more devastatingly than in the May family, once they had received that dreadful telegram in August 1918. Fred May had been a truly faithful and very hard working parish priest. He had ministered to his parishioners, and during the war he had often had to comfort them when the telegrams brought news of injury and death. The list of "killed in action" whom he remembered week by week at his Sunday services grew ever longer. Since April 1917 his own eldest son had been on that list, as a reminder to him that his own family could not be exempt from the dreadful slaughter.

Fred would not have been human if he had not prayed for the safety of his other, remaining, son. The news that Tom had been killed after only two days in France, before he had even reached the front, was a terrible blow to his father. Fred had already jeopardised his health doing the parish Post round during the war, and walking many miles a day in all weathers to deliver the mail. His heart as it turned out was badly strained. Now he had to try and carry on his ministry in the face of this double tragedy. Kate, herself shattered, was in no state to help her husband. The Bishop, Archdeacon and other clergy rallied round to help. It was, fortunately, the school holidays, so Grace, now aged 16, was at home.

It must have been very hard on Grace. First, she had been devoted to both her brothers, as their letters to her show. Those letters she kept and treasured for a further 84 years. But it was even worse for her to see her beloved father, who had always been a rock to her, now in a state of near collapse, mentally and physically. There were two other main

Grace May, c 1920.

considerations. If Fred was forced to give up his ministry through ill health, though only 61 years old, the May family would lose their home and have to move away from Cardynham and all their friends. Also Grace would have to leave Godolphin School, Salisbury, before she had been able to take her school certificate. All hopes of higher education would now be dashed. (In the event, she was later able to travel back to the school to take the exams, which she passed.) There was one small ray of comfort for the family, and that was the presence of uncles, aunts and cousins, some of whom were following successful and quite lucrative careers. The wider family had always admired Fred for the sacrifice he had made in becoming a country parson, and they had already rallied round to pay the necessary school fees for his three children to attend boarding schools. Now they would deeply sympathise with him and his family in their tragedy and illness, and do what they could to help.

Fred was able to soldier on as Rector at Cardynham for several years, greatly helped and supported by friends. Eventually the family decided that a move east would be sensible, but did not want to go too far from friends and relatives, - most living in east Cornwall. Finance had to be a major consideration, and in due course a house for rent was spotted advertised in the village of Tuckenhay. The story was told that Fred travelled up by train to Totnes, and then

Photographs of Fred May and his family taken towards the end of his life, in the mid 1920s.

walked the few very hilly miles to the village. There he slowly climbed the steep front drive, and saw an amazing bed of Christmas Roses in full flower under the dining room window. (It must have been round Christmas time.) Fred was no longer interested in anything else, and took the house on the spot. Fred took his last service at Cardynham on April 26th 1923, and soon after the family moved to Springfield, Tuckenhay, close to the river Dart in South Devon. Tuckenhay is a very picturesque village, set beside Bow Creek, which branches off from the river. One of its main features is a paper mill, giving local employment, and using the clear pure water from a local spring. A millpond and leat provided the head of water for the waterwheel which supplied power to the mill before the coming of the internal combustion engine.

Tuckenhay Mill wharf.

Springfield is a very attractive house, set back from the road in a fairly steeply sloping garden. Unfortunately, before long Fred developed worse heart problems, and the steep hills became a problem, as he had always been a great walker, and now had a large Labrador called Theo to exercise. Kate had never been a great one for walking unlike her daughter Grace, who took after her father.

South Devon proved a beautiful area to live in, and there was a strong Girl Guide organisation which Grace at once became attached to. The only real problem was transport for the family, and here once again Uncle Charles came to the rescue with typical generosity, writing to Grace, now 20 years old, to tell her he had arranged for her to pick up a more modern Model "T" Ford from Harrisons Garage in Totnes at her convenience. A very excited Grace arrived at the garage at the first opportunity, and found the car waiting for her. Mr. Charlie Niles, the proprietor, suggested that a mechanic accompany Grace as she drove a couple of times round the block, getting familiar with the controls. Grace always remembered this sage man saying, in broad Devon, "Donne mind the bends, Miss Grace, but mind the blam fule who come round too fast t'other way!" The mechanic also showed her how to service the engine.

Kate May in her garden, at Springfield c1925

He then drove her gently round the block, and indicated that Grace should take a turn! Grace drove a couple of times round, and then the mechanic waved her goodbye, and she was on her own. The road to Tuckenhay starts with a very steep hill out of Totnes, and continues with more hills until it dives down through Ashprington and so to the steep drive up to Springfield. Grace took it all in her stride! But by then she was a very experienced driver, and not scared of anything on the road.

The arrival of the car marked a whole new exciting chapter in Grace's life, and gave her the ability to take her parents out and about, and to visit relatives and friends. She linked up with the local Guides and Rangers, and soon met Katharine Parker, who lived in rather grand style at Sharpham House, further down river on the west bank of the Dart. Another Guiding friend was Nell Outram, daughter of the vicar of Berry Pommeroy, near Paignton. These three became lifelong friends. None of the three had any prospect of marriage because of the carnage of the First World War.

Nell Outram with 3 dogs at Sharpham House, 1920s.

As Grace strove to build a new and useful life, it was an increasingly sad time for her parents. Fred's mental and physical health did not really improve, and he aged rather quickly. He soon found that the drive to the house was too steep for him to negotiate, even with stops, but help was at hand. Theo the Labrador was trained to go bounding up the drive when his master arrived at the bottom, and Grace would then bring the Ford down to pick up her father. Fred and Kate must have spent much time nursing their memories and regretting the "might have beens." When they had three teenage children they could look forward to them being married and raising their own families in due course. Now the cruel war had shattered all those hopes, for Grace as well as for the boys, and they could never expect to hold a grandchild in their arms. In those bleak years of the 1920s, when the world faced strikes and economic

Katherine Parker & Grace May at Sharpham House.

depression, the personal loss faced by so many millions of families as a result of the war was the greatest burden to bear. The May family were a perfect example of this situation.

Tragically there was worse to come. We cannot be certain of the details, but Grace in later years hinted at a mental condition. It is shattering when an elderly person, beset by mental strain and illness, suffers a notable change in personality. This may take the form of aggressive behaviour of language, as well as dementia and mental confusion. Grace had always been very close to her father, and she now found this new trial particularly hard to bear. Her mother, being by now in her mid-seventies could not cope with it, and needed support as well. Fortunately for Grace by this time she had wonderful friends in Katharine and Nell and others, as well as the continuing support of her family at a distance. For example she was able to exchange the Model "T" Ford for a much newer Morris Cowley, and she no longer had to cope with breakable sparking plugs and valves that had to be "ground in."

After a long illness Frederick May died in 1929, and in many ways his passing must have been a great relief to both Grace and her mother. He was buried in the churchyard at Cardynham Church, close

to the war memorial commemorating the sacrifice made by his two sons. Meanwhile Grace had made another new acquaintance on becoming involved with Devon Girl Guides, and this was Rosia Fleming from Chagford. The two ladies had one experience in common. Rosia had lost her only brother killed in action in 1917, and was now an only child with aging parents. Grace had lost both her brothers in the same way, and was now in a similar

The War Memorial in Cardynham Churchyard.

situation. Despite the fact that Chagford was some way away from Tuckenhay, both of them could drive and had cars, - Rosia's family were quite well off, -and so they soon became good friends. Rosia like Grace was a very practical lass with an adventuresome spirit.

As the 1920s progressed, Rosia had come to an "understanding" with Oliver Tyler, working as a pioneer out in Kenya, that one day when he was ready and had built a house they would be married. Grace must have known all about this arrangement, and in due course when the great day finally came in June 1927 Grace was a bridesmaid at Oliver and Rosia's wedding at Chagford Church, and afterwards at their large house, Millholme, which was nearby. After a lengthy touring honeymoon Rosia left with Oliver for her new home in Kenya, and Grace must have been very sad to see them go.

Rosia Fleming and Grace May, Girl Guides in the 1920s in Devon.

Well within the year Rosia had her first child, and Grace was not to see her again for about five years, when she joined the family who were on holiday at Instow.

While Oliver and Rosia were rebuilding their lives abroad, Grace and her

mother decided to make a move. This may have been for economic reasons, or in order to be nearer to Katharine Parker who had now moved with her mother to Strete Manor, on the eastern end of Slapton Sands. They rented Oddicombe House, in Chillington, a village in the South Hams district of South Devon, and on the road from Dartmouth to Kingsbridge. The new house was only a couple of miles away from the Parkers, along the lovely road across Slapton Sands.

(Above) Oddicombe House, near Chillington, South Devon.

Nell Outram and Katherine Parker at a Guide Camp. 1920s.

Both Katharine and Grace were now making a name for themselves in Guiding circles. In due course Grace would become a Divisional Commissioner and Devon County Camp Advisor, while Katharine Parker reached the summit, becoming County Commissioner for Devon. But that was some way in the future, and meanwhile they were both much involved, with other friends, running both Guides, Brownies and Rangers.

By this time, Kate May was about 80 but in remarkably good health. At Oddicombe there were always unattached cousins to be found, ageing spinsters whose hopes of marriage and family had been ended by the war casualties. Roger May, another cousin, was to lose his father through a tragic cycling accident on the steep hill down to Padstow in north Cornwall. Several of the unattached cousins had no homes of their own, and would later come and stay as "companions" to Kate May as she progressed through her 80s and into her 90s. Grace, now in her 30s, seemed all set to join them in due course, but Grace was tough and found herself plenty of adventurous things to do. In the mid-1930s she and Katharine Parker went on a holiday to the Austrian Tyrol, and stayed at the village inn in the small village of Pettneu, down the river valley from St. Anton. It was a wonderful holiday with walking and mountain climbing, and the Inn Keepers young son, Willie, seems to have acted as guide to the young ladies, an arrangement which was successful on all sides. Pettneu is situated on the main railway line from Switzerland to Innsbruck, so they probably travelled by train. In other parts of the world, like Germany, the 1930's were a time of increasing stress and turmoil, but in England in the early 30s an economic recovery was slowly under way, and with increasing availability of electricity and transport life got a bit easier for many people, especially those living in country districts. In July 1934 Grace's comfortable world was shattered by the terrible news from Kenya. Her great friend Rosia had died just after giving birth to twin sons. Oliver Tyler was now left alone with five children, two of them new born.

Nell Outram & Grace May in Austria in 1935.

Grace May on horseback, 1930s.

Grace May with her mother, in the early 1930s.

CHAPTER 11. EPILOGUE.

When the tragic news reached England family and friends longed to help, but were too far away to do anything. In Kenya friends and neighbours rallied round, and among them was Helen Van Der Weden, who had come out to replace a mother's help who left to marry a local farmer, and whose brother had a farm close by. Helen was a huge source of support, and stayed with the family for the next couple of years. By this time the eldest, Wilfrid was a pupil at nearby St. Andrew's School, Turi, but the tragedy would mean a change in his future schooling.

(Left) Helen Van der Weydon with Jennifer & Diana Tyler at Molo, Kenya in 1934.
(Right) The chapel at St Andrews School, Turi, Elburgon, Kenya, photographed in 2008.

Oliver's mind was in a turmoil. On the one hand there was still much to do in Kenya with the business enterprises, and he did not want to let his loyal partners down. On the other hand, in addition to all the domestic and family challenges and duties, all the fun had gone from the great enterprise, for Rosia had been such a perfect partner for Oliver in every way. What was the point in it all now? All the rebuilding of his life that he had achieved since the end of that ghastly war seemed pointless without his wife.

After discussions with others, and much agonised deliberation, Oliver made the decision. He would sell out to his partners for whatever his share was valued at, and return with his family to England. Later in the 1950s Oliver was to reflect that this was the best decision he ever made. Within five years the Second World War had engulfed the world, and this was followed in Kenya by the Mau Mau troubles in due course, which was a tragic and dangerous period for white settlers

The Dairy at Oliver's farm at Molo, Kenya, 1934

in the country, and this was followed by Independence, and the ejection of most ex-patriots. Charles Millington and Ralph Hoddinott were obliged to leave their life's work in Kenya, taking only what they could carry in a couple of suitcases. When members of Oliver's family visited Kenya in 2009 they found both his house and the saw mill had been destroyed, having most recently suffered in the "troubles" that engulfed the country.

The ruins of Oliver's sawmill in Kenya, seen in 2008.

Oliver received about £30,000, but retained some shares in the company. These in the end proved worthless. This sum would be the equivalent of about £3 million today, 2016. Oliver decided in the early autumn of 1934 to bring his family home to Liverpool by sea, and photographs show them all enjoying the swimming pool on the ship. Helen had also offered to travel with them back to England, and she must have been a great help caring for the five children on the ship. In fact it is doubtful whether Oliver could have managed on his own. One has a feeling that perhaps Helen was hoping for a more permanent relationship in the future, but for some reason this was not to happen.

Wilfrid Tyler with camera, back in England in 1935.

Oliver and his children on board the ship returning to England in 1935.

On arrival back in England Oliver had to take a very hard decision, and that involved splitting up his children while he chose a future home for them. Here there was an echo of the former situation in Kenya, when he had been determined to provide a house and base before inviting Rosia to share it with him. Was this need for security another left over from his experiences in the war and its aftermath? Wilfrid was left in the care of Rosia's aunt in Liverpool. She was a pretty powerful lady who presided over what must have seemed a very forbidding establishment for a boy of 7. Jennifer and Diana went to stay with Walter and Lil at Wormley, which was more relaxed and the two remained together, so had a more agreeable time. The twins, still only a few months old, went to Rosia's mother at Chagford, where they were looked after by the very capable Sister McDonelle. This seems very hard on the children, but it gave the family a chance to feel that they were helping in the tragic situation, and it freed Oliver to decide what to do next, and to make and execute plans for the future of the family. The first question was "where should they settle?" It

Gran Fleming and eldest children 1935

seemed a choice between Hertfordshire, near Oliver's parents, or else South Devon, near Rosia's mother, and Oliver's brother Roland. Ever since he had found South Devon and the Salcombe Estuary Oliver had loved the area, and now he decided that this should be the place where he would settle. He could afford, if he was careful, to live as a retired person, making good use of his capital, so in the early spring of 1935 he began house hunting in earnest.

The house Elm Park, on the outskirts of the village of Broadhempston, had been on the market in 1930 and had not sold. Now, in 1935, the field Nedbury had been sold off separately, and the rest of the house and grounds were again for sale. Oliver was able to buy the property for £2500.

Easter 1935 was a happier time for the family, as they were able to be all together at Chagford with a festival presided over by Rosia's mother, known as Gran Fleming. Now Oliver was busy equipping Elm Park, and he enjoyed collecting furniture from second hand shops. One of his best finds was a slightly damaged dining table of a naval design. He picked it up for £5 from a little shop in Dartmouth, a port

where many of the old "wooden walls" had been eventually broken up, - some having been prison hulks. Oliver

Sale particulars for "Elm Park" Broadhempston, which Oliver Tyler bought as the family home for £2500 in 1935. It is a lovely house today.

later discovered the twin to his dining table in the

Admirals cabin aboard H.M.S. Victory in Portsmouth. Oliver's table had been damaged at the battle of Trafalgar, he suggested!

The dining table on board H.M.S. Victory.

123

In May 1935 the family were able to move into Elm Park, and a whole new chapter in Oliver's life began. The house had 6 bedrooms, and the "annexe" close by, which was a converted stone barn, had six more bedrooms and a large room on the ground floor designed for Admiral Morrison's ex-naval parties! There was a "school room" and range of workshops in the garden, and on the other side of a narrow lane a large garage, stabling, fuel sheds, foodstuff storage and a large woodshed. There was formal garden, two vegetable gardens, two orchards and a two acre paddock, the whole amounting to about eight acres. From the upper floor of the house you can look away to Dartmoor in the north west. Walter and Lil decided to sell their house in Wormley also in 1935, and they moved in to live at Elm Park, being a great help and support to Oliver.

Jennifer Tyler, with Gwen and Frank Cose, Elm Park.

Elm Park, Broadhempston, with the Annexe at Left.

Oliver found Frank and Gwen Cose in the village, and quickly engaged them as gardener/ handyman, and cook. Both were expert and very hardworking, and gave over twenty years of service at Elm Park. Frank was perhaps not fully appreciated until he went off to the war, and the family had to manage without him! Girls from the village took it in turns to be parlour maids, and Nanny Hopkins presided over the children's nursery, and became a lifelong friend of the family.

(Left) Nanny Hopkins with 5 Elder children and a new arrival. Elm Park in 1939.

Oliver soon made friends with the vicar, Dick Evans, a somewhat fiery Welshman with huge talent and a great character, and the three daughters from the vicarage came down to Elm Park to be given lessons with the older Tyler children, Jennifer and Diana, by Miss Holwell who lived in the village. When Wilfrid was old enough to be sent away to boarding school he went to Mount House School in Plymouth, although the school soon transferred to Tavistock on the edge of Dartmoor. The school was to survive a succession of Tyler boys in due course.

(Right) Pupils and staff at Mount House School, Tavistock, Devon.

Oliver set up his main workshop in the garage, and installed the old family lathe which still gave good service. He was quite a proficient wood turner. He also had a well-stocked tool cupboard, which is still in the family, together with many of his favourite tools. For transport Oliver had brought a Hillman 14 Tourer, which was quite a powerful car, rated at 23 horsepower, most necessary for tackling Devon hills with a full load on board. The garage had a very useful pit, and Oliver was able to get underneath his car and do a lot of the essential maintenance himself, which was most convenient, the nearest garage being about three miles away.

Oliver Tyler with his new Hillman 14 Tourer in about 1936

In a letter written to his sister Helen, Walter wrote: "This is a lovely place, and by the appetites everyone gets I think it must be more bracing than Devon generally is; we are on high ground sloping to south and west, and each way we look it is across a valley and hills opposite, westerly a bit of Dartmoor in the far distance. We have been too busy lately to do any outings, except into either Totnes or Newton Abbot shopping, but yesterday Oliver took Lil, 2 elder kids and me to Broadsands, a lovely drive through woody hills and dales, about the finest scenery I have seen since Scotland or Wales; it was a nice sandy bay there, and I had a swim, warm as toast, but the rest thought it might have been cold so only paddled. Altogether this place makes one feel quite baronial, although Lil and I work like farmers, man and wife, which is also what I like. All the kids are loveable little noisy scamps, and are going strong and treat me like a brother, no respect however; I don't seem to get this from youngsters somehow.

Wilfrid, Jennifer, Diana, Norman and Nicholas with transport on Elm Park lawn.

Oliver has a tremendous lot to do. Which is the best thing for him, poor old chap, and altogether I trust we shall go on happily and everyone enjoy themselves as much as I do." Walter even had his own workshop in the "schoolroom "block.

*Oliver fishing on the
river Dart, c 1937*

*Family party including
Mrs Kate May beside
the River Dart c 1938.*

*Walter & Lil Tyler with
Oliver's car c 1938.*

However, as his father hints, it was not all hard work. Oliver found time to take his children down to the nearby River Dart, where they could park the car, cross the little Great Western Railway branch line, and walk along the field beside the river until they came to "Sandy Pool" – a lovely pool with flat rocks and a sandy fringe, ideal for children to dig and make pools and dams while their father fished. Sadly the Dart was never a very good Salmon river, and there were a number of very skilful local poachers who took what fish there were! Oliver also found time to go down to the Salcombe Estuary and sail with his friend Major Hotblack on the latter's 30 foot yawl "Foam."

*"Foam" moored in "The
Bag" at Salcombe in about
1938.*

(Above left) Family party including Oliver on Dartmoor.

There can be no doubt that, as his father's letter implies, that this was indeed a healing time for Oliver, with plenty to do, creative projects on hand, and the children around him. True, he had commitments to both his own parents and to Rosia's widowed and bereft mother, but at least she lived fairly nearby. There was the peace and beauty of the Devon countryside all round him, and he had already fallen in love with Dartmoor, with its wild beauty and its Tors and rivers.

Meanwhile, it did not pass unnoticed that a good looking widower had moved into the area, bought a very pleasant house and property, and established himself with his five children, nanny and staff. There was, it was suggested, only one thing lacking, and that was a mistress of the household. Oliver's sister in law, Sylvia, who had a wicked sense of humour, remarked "The whole hierarchy of the Devon Girl Guides movement set to work to supply this deficiency, and it was a case of every woman for herself!"

(Above left) Sylvia Tyler in the 1920s.

Oliver had known Grace May for probably fifteen years, and she now lived on the direct route from Elm Park to the Salcombe Estuary, so it would have been very natural for him to have called on her. Moreover, there was the problem of Nanny's day off. Nanny Hopkins must have a day off each week, and it would be a great help to Oliver if he could have a deputy nanny on those days. By this time Helen Van Der Weyden had faded into the background, having gone to live in London once Oliver and the family were settled down, and once she realised that a relationship with Oliver was not going to develop.

Oliver and Grace Tyler on the beach at Trevone, N. Cornwall, with Jan the dog.

Grace May, intrepid motorist that she was, thought nothing of motoring up each week to Elm Park, and she much enjoyed looking after the children. Grace was good with children of all ages, and her work with Guides and Brownies gave her a lot of experience, and especially with exciting outdoor activities, like camping, cooking on open fires, and swimming. Having her own car meant she could do expeditions with the children if Oliver had business to attend to. As has been suggested, Oliver and Grace had a lot in common, and their devotion to the children became a very special bond. It was not surprising that they resolved to be married.

Oliver and Grace became engaged in mid-1937, but that was also a very sad time as Walter Tyler developed gastric ulcers, and died. He did however live to see his son's future plans beginning to work out. Meanwhile Grace's mother, Kate May was moved to a house in nearby Ipplepen, so she could be helped when necessary.

Oliver and Grace were married on April 21st 1938 in Stokenham Church, with Jennifer and Diana among the bridesmaids, and a guard of honour consisting of Guides and Rangers. The three grandmothers were all able to attend, and after a reception in the local Church Hall the happy couple left for a touring holiday in Cornwall. Roland was best man at his brother's wedding, and must have welcomed the fact that his brother now had the support of a very capable wife.

The marriage of Oliver Tyler and Grace May, in 1938, with Jennifer and Diana Tyler as two of the Bridesmaids

Roland and Sylvia had lived full time in Portlemouth since 1932, and had the two children, Guy and Shirley. They continued to have business interests in London, including being directors of H.& R Fowler Ltd. Stave Merchants, established in 1832. This may have been a company owned by David Roberts, and linked to his Cooperage. But they were more and more involved in the life of the community. For Roland the experience of the Great War, and his adventures as a dispatch rider must have seemed very far away as he looked out on the beautiful waters of the estuary

Salcombe seen from Roland's house in Portlemouth.

Oliver was also able to call on his cousin, Arthur Hitch, and his wife Billie, who now lived in a beautiful house in Stoke Green, to the north of Slough. This was a very convenient place for Arthur to commute into London, and he had a senior position in a business in the city. He was always a very kind and modest man, - he never used the title "Colonel" which he was more than entitled to, and was a favourite "uncle" to Oliver's family. Sadly, he and Billie had no children so they do not have any descendants today.

All over western Europe there were widows of all ages bereaved in the aftermath of the war. Oliver Tyler now had three grandmothers in that situation. His own mother, Lil, his first wife Rosia's mother, known as Gran Fleming, and his wife Grace's mother, Kate May, known as Gry. All were widows, and all three had lost sons killed in action. Fortunately Gran Fleming, who was completely alone, lived fairly close by at Chagford. She was visited on regular occasions, and delighted in seeing her grandchildren as they grew up. She was also invited every so often to afternoon tea at Elm Park, being driven over in the family limousine. On one such occasion Gran was holding forth to the assembled family, and stretched out her knife and scooped up most of a person's butter ration

The three grandmothers with new arrival Thomas in 1939.

A family party round the dining table at Elm Park.

for a week, but in transferring it to her plate it slipped off her knife and plopped into her cup of tea. Mindful of how precious butter was, she desperately fished in her tea cup, endeavouring to scoop it out, but in vain, while the youngest member of the family, who had been deemed old enough to grace the occasion dissolved into fits of laughter, and had to be hurriedly escorted from the room by his father, trying to conceal his own laughter! I had to remain in the kitchen with my younger siblings It was most convenient having "Gry" in the village of Ipplepen, literally on the route from Elm Park to Newton Abbot, our main local town. The house proved ideal, and calling in was most convenient and enabled help with shopping and other needs to be made much easier. Gry was often brought down to Elm Park to share in family activities, together with

Aunt Olive and her beloved gulls.

"companion cousins" who might be residing with her, and she lived on well into her 90s, until the later 1940s. It proved an ideal arrangement, and went some way to healing the dreadful hurt inflicted by the Great War. Lil Tyler was now very much on her own, though still living at Elm Park. On the principle that two women cannot easily share a kitchen, it was decided to build her a house at Portlemouth, next door to Roland. Her only surviving sister, Olive, had moved down to the Salcombe Estuary, where she lived on a houseboat in Batson Creek, There she lived a very eccentric life breeding sea gulls, and the local boatmen, taking tourist excursions round the harbour, would make sure they included Aunt Olives houseboat. She would take time off from incubating gulls eggs in her bed, put on her best hat and come up on deck to take a bow.

Family group at Ferryhill, with Lil, Oliver and Roland and some of their children.

Unfortunately Aunt Olive had a challenge in the form of the local cats, which would stalk her beloved gulls on the local rubbish dump, conveniently near, and commit murder. She then devised a means of catching the cats, and with the help of a cloth and quantities of chloroform, would act as judge, jury and executioner. It is not surprising that the local Salcombe cat owners discovered what was in the wind, - chloroform is powerful stuff! and decided an end must be made of her campaign. The result of all this was that Roland and Sylvia felt it was expedient to remove their aunt to a place of refuge and safety as soon as possible.

In 1938 Oliver and Roland bought the field up the hill from Ferryside, from Edward Roberts, Sylvia's brother, and they then designed and had built a house for their mother, Lil and Aunt Olive to live in, called Ferryhill. The house was a very attractive one in a superb position looking out over the estuary. Its only real drawback was the steepness of the hill up to the house, and the fact that its garage had to be at the bottom close to the lane which served that part of Portlemouth. This house proved to be the ideal solution, as the two sisters could keep one another company, keeping Aunt Olive away from both gulls and cats, - though she always had a cat of her own, and Roland lived just over the lane from their property, so could keep an eye on them both. Again, this arrangement went a long way to healing the hurt of the loss in the Great War. At Elm Park, the family not only grew in size physically, but also in number, with the arrival of Thomas in mid-1939. He was

The new house built for Lil Tyler in 1938, with Roland's boathouse down below.

132

to be followed by two more brothers and a sister. The next generation of Oliver's descendants, with their marriage partners, numbered 63, and the current total with partners is about 150.

Of those seven men who enlisted to fight in the Great War Oliver Tyler is the only one to have descendants today, and this emphasises once more what a tragedy the war was for so many, many families throughout our country and beyond.

Oliver Tyler - major in the Home Guard, with Thomas, at Elm Park in 1940.

This book attempts, in a very small way, to honour those seven men, and especially the four who were killed in action, but hopefully it will also honour the millions of men whom the seven represent, on both sides of the tragic conflict. As they rest in cemeteries across Europe and beyond, they should never be forgotten.

*A Royal Flying Corps aircraft
over the trenches in France.1917.*